# TEEN DOLLS
## IDENTIFICATION AND VALUE GUIDE

by Patricia R. Smith

Copyright: Patricia Smith, 1977

ISBN NO. 0-89145-051-3

This book or any part thereof may not be reproduced without the written consent of the author and publisher.

Additional books may be ordered at $7.95 from:

**COLLECTOR BOOKS**
P.O. Box 3009
Paducah, Kentucky 42001

## DEDICATION

This little book is dedicated to all the collectors who enjoy and appreciate these fashion dolls of the past 20 years and like collecting them.

PHOTOS BY: Dwight F. Smith
Houston Photos by Phyllis Houston

The following collectors have helped me by loaning some very hard to find teen and pre-teen dolls. Each is acknowledged along with the pictures:

| | |
|---|---|
| Joan Asherbraner | Sharon Hazel |
| Joan Amundsen | Ellie Haynes |
| Joe Bourgious | Phyllis Houston |
| Bessie Carson | Marge Meisinger |
| Louise Ceglia | Jeannie Niswonger |
| Renie Culp | Mary Partridge |
| Marie Ernst | Shirley Peustzer |
| Beverly Gardner | Betty Tait |
| Bessie Greeno | |

OTHER BOOKS BY AUTHOR:

Modern Collector's Dolls, Vol. 1, 2 & 3
Antique Collector's Dolls, Vol. 1 & 2
Armand Marseille's Dolls
Kestner and Simon & Halbig Dolls
Shirley Temple Collectables

## INTRODUCTION

The author would like to thank LaVonne McElroy and Sharon Hazel for their help in compiling this list of known teen and related family dolls. We all agree that this is not a complete listing but only the ones that we have been able to authenticate.

Collectors have been "hoarding" all these teens in the hopes that some day they would be identified and that an accurate price could be set on them. This author finds that there are many exclusive "teen" collectors, who tell me that "it's a matter of room" and they really like the dolls. Other collectors let me know that the teens are "a part of the whole" and they include many into their collections. So we have different reasons for the collectors hanging onto teen dolls.

As to "fair" value being set on the dolls, that is most difficult as they are not on the re-sale market, due to the above stated reasons, so to price these dolls, the author will say this: the quality of the doll is the item used to set the price. Normally not only the quality but the availability and how rare it is figure into the pricing but in these teens, only a few stand out and could be called exceptions. These exceptions include the first Barbie by Mattel, Lilli of West Germany, Alexander's Brenda Starr, Yolanda, Margot, Hasbro's G. I. Jane, Ideal's Super heroines, Joe Namath, etc., and all would bring over $20.00. So to price the dolls in this book, we will say this: any doll that does not show a price after the name in the following list, is worth less than $1.00.

If you are a seamstress and have any teens that you really do not want to keep, our suggestion would be to dress them and if you are a really fine seamstress, dress them as "historical personalities" and donate them to your school system to be used as visual aids in any area they desire. Another suggestion would be to donate them to your local Girl Scouts and Brownies, or Campfire Girls, to be used for activities, sales, promotions or awards. There are many, many patterns available to dress these teens in fashions from a great many eras.

Dolls marked with an * are shown in this book. Others may be found in MODERN COLLECTOR'S DOLLS, SERIES I, II, or III. See listing following name where they may be found, plus current values.

**3" - 6": All are dressable and most have movable joints.**
 3" Bridal Shower Favor - Japan.
 3½" Jodi - Merry Mfg. $1.00.
 3½" Fashion Teeners - Mattel. Coreen/Doreen/Loreen/Moreen. $6.00 each. (See Mattel Section, Series III)
 4½" Name unknown - Japan. Early 1960's. Good quality hard plastic. Sleep eyes. High heels. Ponytail hairdo.
 5" Matchbox Dolls. Lesney of England. Party Patty/Sailor Sue—Alice in Wonderland/Jodphur. $4.00 each. (See Lesney Section, Series III.) 1974.
* 5" Suky - Lesney of England. Complete wardrobe available. Still available.
 5" Flying Nun - Hasbro. $12.00. (See Series I, page 131.)
 5" Ballerina & Stewardess Series - Imperial Toy Corp. $2.00. (See Series II, page 165.)
* 5" Tiny Teens - Uneeda. $4.00. (See Series II, pages 310, 311.)

**6" - 7": Fashion Dolls.**
* 6" Barbra - Playmate. $4.50.
* 6" Dorable Doree - Jilmar Co. $2.00. (Dawn type).
* 6" Diana - unknown $4.00. (Dawn doll).
* 6" Tiny Tina - Totsy Toy. $3.00.
* 6¼" Debbie Teen - Maker unknown. $2.00.
* 6" - 6½" Dawn and Friends - Topper Corp/Deluxe Topper. 1st Series: Angie ($5.00), Dale* ($6.00), Dawn* ($4.00) & Glori* ($5.00), (3 boys: See male listing), 1970. Later added: Jessica* ($5.00), Longlocks* ($6.00), and dancing: Same plus Fancy Feet* ($5.00) and 4 boys (See male listing); Majorettes: Dawn ($8.00), Connie ($8.00), Kip* ($8.00) and April* ($8.00), Model Agency: Dawn ($8.00), Denise ($8.00), Dinah ($8.00), Daphne ($8.00), Melanie ($8.00), Maurine ($8.00). Head to Toe: Dawn ($5.00), Angie ($5.00) and Longlocks ($5.00). (See Series II, pages 62-69.)
* 6½" Cindy Joy - Mort Alexander (White and suntan. At least two versions.) $1.50.
* 6½" Judy - Day-Fran. $1.00.
* 6½" Fashion World - Dandee Doll Mfg. Corp. $1.50.
 6½" Miss Price - Horsman. Bedknobs & Broomsticks. $10.00. (See Series II, page 144.)

6½" Little Miss Dollikin - Uneeda. $3.00. (See Series II, page 313.)
* 7½" Dinah-Mite - Mego Corp. 2 versions. White & black. $4.00. (See Series II, page 270).
* 7½" Jeanie - Kresge Co. $1.00.
* 7½" Marcia Ann - Standard Doll Parts. $3.00.

## 8" - 8½": Fashion Dolls
Cara - Plymouth. $3.00.
Dancers - Flagg. Also Internationals and Historicals. $7.00. (See Series II, page 95.)
* Derry Daring - Ideal. 1975. Still Available.
* Diana - Hong Kong. $6.00. (Fashion doll with poodle.)
* Dress Me's - Hasbro. /Lingerie Lou by Duchess/Princess Ann/Marcie, etc. $2.00 each. (See Series I, page 242.)
Flatsy Teens - Ideal. Ali/Dale/Cory/Gwen. 1970. $3.00. (See Series I, page 176.)
* Gina Teenager - Allison Corp. $4.00.
Go-Go Girls - Deluxe Reading. 8 in series. $5.00. (See Series I, page 63.)
* High Heel Teen - Virga. 1957. $6.00.
Jackie Twist Waist - Fun World.
* Jenny Jones - Kenner. $8.00.
* Judi - Belle. $3.00.
Little Miss Dollikin - Uneeda $3.00. (Original issue of Triki Miki).
* Little Miss Ginger - Cosmopolitan. $6.00.
* Little Shopper.
Marcie Ann - Hong Kong.
* Margaret - Japan (larger head size) $1.50.
Mary Lou - Fab-Lu-Ltd. Tammy type. 1964. $2.00.
Mini Fashion - Dandee. $1.00.
Mod Miss - Edico Products. $1.00.
* Nikki - Hong Kong. $1.50.
* Penny Street - Japan. $5.00.
Rockflowers - Mattel. 5 in series: Heather/Lilac/Rosemary/Iris & Doug. $4.00. (See Series II, pages 256 and 257.)
Sandra Sue - Richwood Co. $12.00. (See Series III, Richwood Section.)
Standard Doll Co. - Hong Kong.
Sweet 16 Cake Decoration - Hong Kong.
Triki Miki - Uneeda. (Formerly Little Miss Dollikin) $3.00.
Walking Teenager. Jointed knees, head turns - Maker unknown. 1957. $4.00.
? Name unknown - Marx. Slightly larger than Dawn. $1.50.

? Name unknown - Marx. Rubbery, with painted-on shoes/boots. $1.00.
? Name unknown - Mego.

**9" - 9½": Little Miss Teens and others.**
* Betty - Marx. One of the Archie series. Still available.
* Betty Boots - Jak Pak. $2.00.
  Bonnie Breck - Hasbro. $10.00. (See Series II, page 136.) 1971.
* Bonnie Jean - Japan. $7.00.
* Candi - Maker unknown. $6.00.
  Candy - Spiegels. Polly's sister. 1964. $3.00.
* Carla - Mego. $2.00.
  Carla - Peggy Ann Doll Clothes. $3.00.
  Collette - Hong Kong. 1971. $7.00. (See Series III, Page 146).
* Daisy - Gabriel. 1974. Still available.
  Debbie Eve - Skippy Doll Co. 1965. $6.00.
* Dr. Russell - Mattel. Still available.
  Jenny - A. T. C. - Admiration Toy Co. $6.00.
* Jody - Ideal. Four in series. Pioneer/Victorian/Gibson Girl/Country Girl. 1975 & 1976. Still available.
* Lorraine - Playmate. $8.00.
  Little Miss Ginger - Cosmopolitan. $8.00. (See Series II, page 58.)
* Liza Jane - Hong Kong. $1.50.
  Michella Ann - Aldens. 1972. Jointed waist, short bob hair. $2.00.
  Minnerette - Uneeda. Several versions. $4.00.
  Mother to Cheerful Family - Lincoln International (See Series III, page 194). Still available.
* Mother Hattie Happy - Mattel. Still available.
  Mother Rider - Hong Kong (RT). Still Available.
  Mother Springtime Family - Made for Kresge. (See Series III, page 270). Still available.
  Mother Steffie Sunshine - Mattel. (Series II, page 56). Still available.
  Peggy - Peggy Ann Doll Clothes Co. 1964. $3.00.
* Police Girl - L.J.N. Four in series: Nurse, Forest Ranger, Highway Patrol, and Police). Still available.
* Policewoman - Horsman. 1976. Still available.
  Pretty Quix - Paper Bodies. 2 girls, 1 boy. $7.00 set. (See Series III.)
* Sister - Hasbro. $1.00.
* Veronica - Marx. One of Archie group. Still Available.
* Wanda - Shindana. 1st. Issue - $9.00. Also white version, $9.00. 1972. (See Series II, page 298.)

World of Love - Hasbro. (See Series I, page 143 and Series II, page 133.) Five in Series:Music, $9.00, Peace, $5.00, Flower, $5.00, Soul, $5.00, Love, $5.00.

**10" - 10½": Teen Girls.**
* Annette Funicello - Uneeda. 1961. $10.00.
* Ballerina - Valentine. 11VW mark. 2 versions at least. $5.00.
  Belinda - NASCO. $10.00.
* Blue Fairy - Uneeda. From Pinocchio. (See Series I, page 283.) $4.00.
* Bonita - Sayco. $12.00.
  Bonnie - Allied. $6.00.
* Bride - Plastic Molded Arts. 1957. $3.00.
* Carol - Commonwealth (Several styles) (See Series II, Page 57.) $6.00.
* Chiltern girl from England - Name unknown. $8.00.
  Cindy - Horsman. 1957. $9.00.
  Cissette - Madame Alexander. (See Series II, Page 21, and Series I, page 21.) $25.00.
* Coty Girl - Arranbee Doll Co. Also called Miss Coty. Marked ⊗ and Ⓟ $6.00.
  Cycling Cheri - Tomy (See Series II, page 303.) Still available.
* Debbie Ballerina - Hong Kong. $4.00.
* Debbie - Mayfair, Canada. $5.00.
  Fashion Model - Maker unknown. 1962. $4.00.
* Francine Fairy Tale Doll - Maker unknown. 1957. $6.00.
* Gigi Perreau - A & H Doll Co. (See "Miss"). $12.00.
  Happy Time - Montgomery Ward. Mark: Ⓟ. 1961. $5.00.
  Hi-Heel Ballerina - Jointed waist, on plastic stand - Valentine, 1957. $9.00.
* Jan - Vogue. 1959. (See Series I, page 297.) $15.00.
  Jacqueline - Madame Alexander. (See Series I.) $75.00.
* Jenny - A. T. C. (See photo "Wendy"). $6.00.
* Jill - Vogue. 2 versions. Hard plastic and vinyl. 1959. (See Series I, page 297.) $15.00.
* Judy - Maker unknown. Mark: X. 1958. Bubblecut and 1-pc. body, arms and legs. $5.00.
  Judy Joyful - Hong Kong. $4.00.
  June Bride - Maker unknown. All vinyl with jointed waist. 1958. $4.00.
* Kay - Eegee. 1960. Also marketed as Miss Patti. $15.00.
  Latest Fashion - Hong Kong. $3.00.
* Laurie - Plaything. All vinyl. Walker, head turns. 1958. $7.00.
  Leggys - Hasbro. Sue/Nan/Jill/Kate. (See Series II, page 135.) $5.00.
* Little Miss Marie - Made for Woolworth. $6.00.

* Little Miss Nancy Ann - Nancy Ann Doll Co. (See Series I, page 236.) $6.00.
* Little Miss Revlon - Ideal. 1957. (See Series I, page 164.) $14.00.
* Little Sister - Hong Kong. $3.00.
  Make-Ur-Own Doll - Cosmopolitan. (See Series III, Page 55.) $8.00.
* Maxi-Girl - Maker unknown. $6.00.
  Maxi-Mod - M & S Shillman. 1973. (See Series II, page 297.) $4.00.
* Miss Coty - Arranbee. 1958. Also called Coty Girl. $6.00.
* Miss Gigi Perreau - A & H. $12.00.
* Miss Ginger - Cosmopolitan. Also called Little Miss Ginger. $7.00.
  Miss Laurie - Active Doll Corp. Mindy's big sister. $6.00.
  Miss Laurie - Natural Toy Corp. $6.00.
* Miss Marie - Made for Woolworths. Also called Little Miss Marie. $6.00.
* Miss Nancy Ann - Nancy Ann Doll Co. Also called Little Miss Nancy Ann. $6.00.
* Miss Ritzi - Natural Doll Co. Mark: E .$6.00.
* Miss Teena - Horsman. Yvonne Doll Division. 1961. $8.00.
* Miss Vicky - Elite Creations, by Unique. $1.50.
  Miss Vicky - Mary Hoyer Doll Co. $9.00.
* Missy - Plastic Molded Arts. $1.50.
* Penny - Flagg Doll Co. $12.00.
* Pink Fairy - Uneeda. From Babes in Toyland. $4.00.
* Pollyanna - Uneeda, 1961. $20.00.
* Rosemary - Rosemary Doll Co. Marks: P . $5.00.
  Rosemary Ballerina - Mark: P . $8.00.
  Sally - Maker unknown. All vinyl, white hair, unjointed waist. 1958. $4.00.
  Shapely Teen - Maker unknown. All vinyl. Unjointed waist. 1959. $4.00.
* Sherry - Eegee. $4.00.
* Suzette - Uneeda. Both with painted eyes and sleep eyes. Molded and rooted hair. $5.00.
* Teenage Shirley Temple - Ideal. (NOT marketed as S. T. Factory put-together.) 1956. $15.00.
  Teenager - Yvonne-Horsman. Jointed waist and knees. 1959. $8.00.
  Teeny Bopper - Toy House. $1.00.
* Tina Ballerina - Valentine. Mark: 11VW. 2 styles. $8.00.
  Tiny Teen - Uneeda. (See Series I, page 283.) 1957-60. $5.00.
* Toni - American Character. 1958. (See Series II, page 47.) $25.00.
* Wendy - Active Toy Corp. $3.00.

**11" - 12" Slim Teens.**
* Action Girl - Politoy, England. $22.00.
  Action Nurse Jane - Hasbro. $25.00.
* Alice - Hong Kong. Takes wigs. $2.00.
* Aline - Nancy Ann Doll Co. $9.00.
* Aloha Alice - Hong Kong. $5.00.
* Anita - GIG. Still available.
  Annette - Eegee. Rooted hair as well as wigs. $6.00.
* Babe - Hong Kong. World French pavillion doll. $125.00 up.
* Babette - Eegee. Also called Miss Babette. $6.00.
* Babette - Hong Kong. $4.00.
  Babs - Fab-U-Ltd. $4.00.
  Babs - Maker unknown. Girl friend of Bob. Aldens. 1964. $1.00.
* Ballerina Nita - Roberta. $6.00.
* Barbara Jo - New Dolly Toy Co. 1965. $4.00.
* Barbie - Mattel. (See Series II, pages 187-267).
  Batgirl - Ideal. (See Series III). $22.00.
* Betsy Teen - Hong Kong. Many versions. Made for Mont. Ward. 1970. $2.00.
  Bette - Hong Kong
* Betty - Aldens. 1962. $4.00.
* Betsy Teen - Maker unknown. $4.00.
  Bonita - Maker unknown. $1.00.
* Botique - Peggy Ann Doll Clothes Co. Both White & Black. Still available.
  Brenda Starr - Madame Alexander. (See Series II, page 20.) $45.00.
  Calamity Jane - Azark-Hamway. (See Series III, page 35.) $5.00.
  Calamity Jane - Excel. (See Series III, page 125). $7.00.
* Cara - Mattel. 1975.
  Carol Channing - AE. Also ponytail style. (See Series II, page 180). $15.00.
  Casey - Mattel. (See Series I, page 203.)
* Charly - Durham. Still available.
* Cherie - Totsy. Made for J. C. Penny. $4.00.
  Christie - Mattel. (See Series III).
* Coast to Coast Girl - Coast to Coast Stores. $8.00.
  Cragston Model - Cragstan. $2.00.
* Dear Judy - Hong Kong. $4.00.
  Debbie - Empire Made. Rooted hair and wigs. $1.00.
* Debbie - Valentine. 1958. $5.00.
  Debbie - Uneeda. $4.00.
* Debbie Drake - Valentine. 1963. $10.00.
* Debbie Pose - Valentine. $8.00.
  Debbie's Sister - Empire Made. $1.00.

* Doll Craft Doll - Hong Kong. $2.00.
  Dolls Parts Doll - Doll Parts Co. $1.50.
* Donna - Action Toy Co. $2.00.
  Dress Me Fashion Teen - Grants Plastics. (See Series I, page 128.)
  Dr. Ben Casey's Nurse. 1963. $9.00.
  Dr. Kildare's Nurse - Japan. $6.00.
  Emma Peel - Pedigree, England. (See Series III, page 142.) $18.00.
* Fashion Teens - Altmans. 1972. $3.00.
* Francie - Mattel. Also Black. (See Series 2, page 197.)
  Generation Family - Hong Kong. Spiegels. Mother and Grandmother are Mindy Pose. (See Series III, page 143). $25.00 set.
* Gina - Allison Corp. $8.00.
* Gigi - Natural Doll Co. $4.00.
* Girl Doll - Hong Kong. Goes with "Boy" doll. $2.00.
* Gloria - Japan. $1.50.
* Go Go Gail - Metropolitan (?). $8.00.
  Grant's Suzette - Hong Kong. Made for Grant Co.
* Groovy Girl - Peggy Ann Doll Clothes Co. $2.00.
  Grown Sister - Maker unknown. Bangs tight to side. 1962. $1.00.
  Haddie Mod - Mego. (See Series I, page 211.) $4.00.
  Honey West - Gilbert. Played by Anne Francis. (See Series II, page 128). $15.00.
* Hot Pants - Hong Kong. $1.00.
* Howard Johnson Waitress - Maker unknown. $9.00.
* Jamie - Mattel. (See Series II, page 198).
  Janie - Laramie. (Also called Wiggy or Mod Judy). $1.50.
* Julia - Mattel (Diahann Carroll).
  Kay - Maker unknown.
* Kelley - Mattel. (See Series II, page 198).
  Kiki Teen - Penco. $1.50.
  Laurie Jane - Hong Kong. Several versions. $1.00.
* Laurie Lee - Ross. $2.00.
* Lili - West Germany. (See Series III). 1958. $100.00 up.
  Lily - Hong Kong. Several versions. 1967-68. (See Series I, page 112). $4.00.
* Linda - Hong Kong (made for Deluxe of Germany). $6.00.
* Linnette - Hone Kong. Made for Australia. $4.00.
* Liz - Louis Greenburg. $1.50.
* Liza Jane - Hong Kong. $1.50.
* Lori - Totsy. $3.00.
* Maddie Mod - Mego. 1968. (See Series I, page 113). $4.00.
  Manikin - Valentine. 1958. Plastic with vinyl head. Full joints. $4.00.

' Marcie Mod - A & H Doll Co. $2.00.
Mariclare - Hong Kong. For J. C. Penny. (See Series 2, page 106). $4.00.
* Marlene - Marx. 1964. $4.00.
* Marzie - Allied. $1.00.
* Maxi-Mod - M & S Shillman. White & Black versions. $3.00.
* Melissa - Hong Kong. Several versions. Mortoys. $1.50.
Michelle - Hong Kong. Several versions.
* Midge - Mattel. (See Series II, page 209).
* Millie - Evergeen. $2.00.
Mindy Mod - Jilmar. $1.00.
Mindy Pose - Aldens. Also Mother and Grandmother of Generation Family. Also Polly's Friend. 1972. $4.00.
Mini Mod - M & S Shillman.
Miss America - Mattel. (See Series II).
* Miss Babette - Eegee, 1961. $6.00.
* Miss Camay - Camay Doll Co. $5.00.
* Miss Fancy - Japan. A. T. C. $4.00.
Miss Fashion - Spiegels.
* Miss Free & Easy - L.J.N. 1975. Still available.
* Miss Free & Easy - Zayre. Still available.
* Miss Petite Fashion - L.J.N. Still available.
Miss Ponytail - Maker unknown. 1967. Jointed waist. $1.00.
* Miss Space Needle - Uneeda. $9.00.
* Miss Teenager - Evergeen. $6.00.
Miss Twist - M & S Shillman. 1967. $2.00.
Miss Universe - Ideal. $10.00.
* Miss World Fashion - Spiegels. One of Polly series. $6.00.
Mitzie - Ideal. (See Series II, page 152). $8.00.
* Miti - Reliable of Canada. $4.00.
* Mod Judy - Hong Kong. Also Janie, Wiggy, Valerie. Made for Australia. (See Series III, page 143).
* Modern Miss - Edico. $2.00.
* Molly - Mytoy Co. 1966. $2.00.
Morton's Frozen Foods Majorette - Maker unknown. $6.00.
* Ms. Bobbi - Walco. 1975. Still available.
* Ms. Toni - Walco. 1975. Still available.
New Fashion - Hong Kong.
Nikki - Maker unknown. Bangs pulled to right. 1964. $1.00.
Nina Ballerina - Tomy (See Series III). Still available.
* Pamela - Brechner. $2.00.
* Pauline - Hong Kong. $2.00.
Penny - P & N. $1.00.
* Petite - L.J.N. Still Available.
* Petite Fashion - Hong Kong. Still available.
* P.J. - Mattel. (See Series II, page 267).

- * Polly Series - Some by Jilmar. Made for Aldens & Spiegels. 1962 to date.
    - Pose, 1967. $5.00.
    - Pose 'N Curl. $4.00.
    - Walker. $3.00.
    - Talker. $6.00.
    - Turner (hair changes color). 1975. Still available.
    - Bride. $3.00.
    - Dance and Rock. 1971. $4.00.
    - Fashion Model. 1965. $4.00.
    - Pose & Walk. 1969. $5.00.
    - Living. $3.00.
    - Curl & Twirl. 1971. $3.00.
    - Rides a bike. $4.00.
    - Flip and Turn. $3.00.
    - World Fashion. $6.00.
    - Grow Hair. 1970. $4.00.
- Pool Dolls. (See Series III, page 144).
- * Pop's Girl - Hong Kong. $2.00.
- * Posey - Jewel Tea Co. Made by Valentine & Marx. $6.00.
- * Pretty Miss - Hong Kong. 1966. $1.50.
- Princess Grace Doll Co., Name unknown. (Part of Mego Corp). $1.00.
- * Rainbow Girl - Hong Kong. $4.00.
- Randy Rider - Maker unknown. Still available.
- Real Model - Maker unknown. Hard plastic walker. 1st small teen. 1956. $9.00.
- Renee - Hong Kong. $1.50.
- * Scarlet - Japan. $10.00.
- Sears Exclusive. Full bangs, long ponytail. Striped bathing suit. 1961. $4.00.
- Shelly Grow Hair - Maker unknown. 1964. $3.00.
- * Sindy - Pedigree, England. 4 versions. Still available.
- * Stacey-Mattel. (See Series II, page 197).
- Standard Doll - Standard Doll Co. $1.50.
- * Steffie - Mattel. (See Series II, page 198).
- * Stiljoy - Sebino, Italy. 1975. Still available.
- * Sunkissed Boutique - Peggy Ann Doll Clothes Co. Still available.
- * Susie - Hong Kong. $1.50.
- * Suzette - Brothers Import. $2.00.
- * Suzzette - Uneeda, both sleep ($8.00) & Painted eyes. ($5.00). (See Series II, page 305).
- * Swinging Sally - Hong Kong. At least 2 versions. $1.50.
- Tanya - Mego for Kresge. (See Series II, page 268). $4.00.
- * Taylor Jones - Ideal. (Black Tuesday Jones). 1976. Still available.

Teena - Maker unknown. 1953. (See Series I, page 221). $4.00.
Teenage Doll - Spiegel.
Teenage Susy - Maker unknown. Plastic with vinyl head. 1964. $1.00.
Texaco Cheerleader - Hong Kong. (See Series II, page 109). $6.00.
Three Generation Family - Hong Kong. (See Series III). $25.00 set.
* Tina - Maker unknown. Hong Kong. $1.50.
* Tina Marie - Woolworths. Marked with U. $3.00.
* Trendi - Hong Kong. $1.50.
Truly Scrumptious - Mattel. Sally Ann Howe. (See Series II, pages 53 & 242).
* Tuesday Taylor - Ideal. 1976. Still Available.
Twiggy - Mattel. British model. 1967. (See Series II, page 218).
* Twistie - Totsy. Several versions. $2.00.
* Valerie - Dantex. $2.00.
* Valerie - Hong Kong. Also called Mod. Judy. $1.00.
Veronique - Hong Kong.
Wakiki Girl - Maker unknown. (See Series II, page 106). $5.00.
Walking Ballerina - Maker unknown. $4.00.
Walking Grown Up - Maker unknown. $2.00.
* Ward's Maddie Mod - Mego. $5.00.
Wendy - Unique. $1.50.
Wendy Ward - Uneeda. For Mont. Ward. Sleep eyes. Takes wigs. 1964. $10.00.
* Wiggy - Laramie. Also called Janie & Mod Judy. $1.50.
Yolanda - Madame Alexander. $45.00.

**11" - 12½": Heavier proportions.**
* American Airlines - same as Mary Make-Up. American Character. $8.00.
Betsy McCall - McCall Corp. (See Series II, page 54). $22.00.
* Calico Lass - Unique. (See Series II, page 316). $4.00.
Candy - American Character. Larger Tressy version. $10.00.
* Cher - Mego. 1976. Still available.
Cinderella - Horsman. (Rich and Poor heads & outfits. See Series II, page 140). $5.00.
Dress Me - Grants Plastics. 1 pc. body & legs. 1969.
* Dusty - Kenner. 1974. Still available.
* Ellie May Clampett - Unique. (See Series II, page 316. $4.00.
* Fifi - Hong Kong. Made for Australia. $3.00.
Flying Nun - Hasbro. $8.00.
* Fullerette - Hong Kong. (For fuller Brush Co.) $10.00.
Gerri - AE. Lorna's sister. $1.00.

* Jamie Sommers, Bionic woman. Kenner. 1976. Played by Lindsey Wagner. Still available.
* Jan - Vogue. $15.00.
* Jennifer - C. G. Morgan Co. 2 styles. Rooted & Grow hair. $6.00.

  Lissy - Madame Alexander. (See Series II, page 17). $45.00.
* Liza Jean - Furga, Italy. $9.00.

  Lorna - AE. Gerri's Sister. $1.00.

  Marjie - Maker unknown.
* Mary Make-up - American Character. (See airline stewardess this listing).

  Mary Poppins - Horsman. 2 issues. (See Series I, page 145). 1965 and 1975. $18.00.

  Mera - Ideal. Queen of Atlantis. 1967. $22.00.
* Merlena - Sharing. $6.00.
* Mia - Bonomi, Italy. $12.00.
* Miss Chelsea - Politoy, England. $4.00.
* Misty, Clairol - Ideal. 2 versions. 1963. (See Series I, page 170). $8.00.
* Mitzi - Reliable, Canada. $5.00.

  Mom - Ideal. To Tammy family. (See Series II, page 155). $12.00.

  Pamela. Alexander Doll Co. $45.00.
* Pamela - Dan Brechner & Co. 1975. $1.00.
* Patty Duke - Horsman. 2 versions. 1965. $16.00.
* Popi - American Doll & Toy Co. $9.00.
* Posin' Tammy - Ideal. $8.00.
* Princess Patty - Canada. $6.00.

  Randy - Fab-U-Ltd. $1.00.
* Ratti Teenager - Italy. $6.00.
* Real Model - Plastic Molded Arts. $3.00.
* Rena - Grants. 2 versions. Rooted and glued hair. $4.00.

  Samantha - Ideal. 1965. (See Series II, page 156). $12.00.

  Shelly - Eegee. (See Series II, page 85). $4.00.
* Skye - Kenner, 1974. Still available.

  Standard Jr. Teen - Standard Doll Co. $1.00.
* Supergirl - Ideal. 1967. $22.00.
* Tammy - Ideal. 1962. Black. $12.00.

  Tammy, Grown up. - Ideal. 2 versions. (See Series II, page 155). $8.00.

  Tammy, Posen' - Ideal. 1964. $8.00.
* Teenage Doll - Maker unknown. Trunk/wardrobe. 1963. $3.00.

  Terry - Spiegels. 1964. $1.00.
* Tina Cassini - Oleg Cassini. 3 hair colors. 1964. $12.00.
* Tressy - American Character. 1963. (See Series I, page 42). $12.00.

Valerie - Hong Kong; also Mod Judy. $1.00.
Vicki/June - Pedigree, England. Sindy's friend. $8.00.
Vicki Teen - Elite Creations by Unique. (See Series II, page 316). $3.00.
* Viviana - Italy. Still available.
* Wonder Doll - Jack Pak. $2.00.
Wonder Woman - Ideal. 1967. $22.00.
? Name unknown - Horsman (may be Cindy). $4.00.
? Name unknown - Plastic Molded Arts (may be Peggy). $2.00.
? Name unknown - Reliable of Canada (may be Tammy). $3.00.
? Name unknown - Marked S. D. Super Doll Co. $4.00.

**12½" - 17": Teens proportioned to fit this section.**
* Barbara Striesand - Japan. $35.00.
Betsy McCall - (See Series I, page 41). $15.00.
Carol Brent - Ideal. $20.00.
Gemette - Eegee. (See Series I, page 78). $4.00.
Judy Littlechap - Remco. (See Series II, page 289). 1963. $15.00.
Lisa Littlechap - Remco. (See Series II, page 289). 1963. $20.00.
Liz - Ideal. (See Series II, page 153). $8.00.
Magic Meg - Uneeda. (See Series II, page 313). $6.00.
Miss Debbie - Eegee. (See Series II, page 84). $6.00.
Miss 17 - Marx. (see Series II, page 185). $10.00.
Pageant Dolls - Kaystan: Miss America, 1970-71. (See Series II, page 167). $25.00.
   Miss Teenage America, 1972.
Shelly - Maker unknown. (See Series II, page 179). $2.00.
* Toni - Ideal. $20.00.
* Toni Walker - American Character. $22.00.

**BOY FRIENDS, BROTHERS AND/OR FATHERS.**
10" Adam - Hasbro. World of Love Group. (See Series II, page 133). $6.00.
12" Adam - Spiegels. Polly's boyfriend. 1969. Posin' Adam, 1972. $2.00.
12" Allen - Mattel. Ken's buddy. (See Series II, page 212).
12" Andy - Eegee. 2 versions. Annette's boyfriend (See Series I, Page 77). $5.00.
* 9" Archie - Marx, 1975. Still available.
12" Beau - Standard girl's boyfriend. $5.00.
12" Ben - Mont. Ward's Betsy's boyfriend. $6.00.
* 12½" Bill - Bella Hess. 1966. $4.00.
* 12" Bill Champ - Totsy. $4.00.
* 12" Bob - Aldens. Bab's Boyfriend. 1964. $3.00.

* 12" Bob - Aldens. Betty's boyfriend. 1963-64. $2.00.
* 12" Bob - Uneeda. Suzette's boyfriend. (See Series I, page 286). $6.00.
  12" Bobby - Laramie. Janie's boyfriend. $4.00.
* 12" Bobby Orr - Royal Toy. Still available.
* 12" Boy Doll - Hong Kong. Girl's boyfriend. $2.00.
  12" Brad - Mattel. Christie's boyfriend. (See Series II, page 198).
* 12" Chuck - Totsy. Cherie's boyfriend. $8.00.
* 12" Cowboy - Hong Kong. $2.00.
  12" Curtis - Mattel. Cara's boyfriend. 1975.
  10" Dad - Kresge. To Springtime Family. Still available.
  10" Dad - Lincoln. To Cheerful Family (See Series III, page 194). Still available.
  13" Dad - Ideal. Tammy's father. 1963. $12.00.
  12" Dad - Sunshine Family. Still available.
  12" Dad - Happy Family. Still available.
  12" Dad - To Rider Family. Still available.
* 11¾ Danny Pose - Alden's & Spiegel's. $4.00.
* 8" David - Hong Kong. Unknown. $8.00.
  12" Don - Alden's & Spiegels. Polly & Betty's boyfriend, 1964. $2.00.
* 8" Don - Mego. Dinah-Mite's boyfriend. (See Series II, page 268). $4.00.
  8" Doug - Mattel. To Rockflower group.
  12" Dr. Ben Casey - with nurse. 1963. $8.00.
* 12" Dr. Kildare - Japan. Doctor & nurse. $4.00.
* 15" Dr. Littlechap - Remco. Husband & father. (See Series II, page 289). 1963. $20.00.
  8" Flagg boys - Flagg. Dancing partners. $4.00.
  7" Gary - Deluxe Topper. Dawn's friend. (See Series II, page 64). $5.00.
* 12" Gary - Maker unknown. $3.00.
* 10" George - Natural. Boyfriend to Jennifer. $6.00.
* 11" Hal - Mattel. To Happy Family. Still available.
* 12" Happening Hank - Peggy Ann Doll Clothes. Groovy Girl's boyfriend. $12.00.
* 11" Jeff - Vogue. Jill's boyfriend. 1959. (See Series I, page 297). $15.00.
  12" Jerry - Hong Kong. Judy's boyfriend. $4.00.
* 9" Jughead - Marx. Still available.
* 12" Ken - Mattel. Barbie's boyfriend. (See Series II, page 212).
  11½" Mod Jerry - Mate for Mod Judy - Australia. (See Series III, page 143). $2.00.
* 12" Paul - Alden's & Spiegels. Polly's twin brother. 1969. Posin' Paul, 1971. $3.00.

12" Pool Doll - (See Series III, page 144). $3.00.
* 7½" Pete - Ideal. Tammy's brother. (See Series II, page 155). $7.00.
* 12" Randy - Totsy. Twistie's boyfriend. $3.00.
* 9½" Ricky - Mattel. Skipper's friend. (See Series II, page 197).
12" Robbie - Spiegels. Polly's boyfriend with flocked hair. $3.00.
12" Rod - J.C. Penney. Mariclare's boyfriend. $3.00.
* 12" Roger - Japan. Unknown. $6.00.
7" Ron - Deluxe Topper. Dawn's group. (See Series II, page 64). $5.00.
10" Steve - Mattel. To Sunshine Family. (See Series II, page 56).
13" Ted - Ideal. Tammy's brother. (See Series I, page 168). $8.00.
* 11½" Toni - Hong Kong. $2.00.
12" Tommy - Maker unknown. 1964. $2.00.
7" Van - Deluxe Topper. Dawn's group. (See Series II, page 64). $6.00.

**5" to 10": PRETEEN BOYS AND GIRLS.**
Alexanderkins - Madame Alexander. (See Series II, page 17). $12.00 to $35.00.
Betsy McCall - American Character & Uneeda. (See Series II, page 54). $22.00.
Bonnie - Bella Hess. Skipper type. 1966. $1.50.
* Candi - Little Sisters. Hong Kong. $2.00.
Candi, New - Little Sisters. Hong Kong. $1.50.
* Carla - Mattel.
Carrie - Marked S. D. Super Doll Co. (See Sries II, page 301). $4.00.
* Chris - Mattel. (See Series II, page 197).
Cricket - Amer. Character. With and without grow hair. (See Series II, page 45). $10.00.
Dodi - Ideal. Plain leg & "posin' " legs. (See Series II, page 155). $7.00.
Dolly Darling Series - Hasbro. (See Series II, page 131). $2.00.
Donna Fashion — Uneeda. (See Series II, page 313). $4.00.
* Doris - Prima. $2.00.
* Dottie - Alden's. $2.00.
Fran - Heidi copy with freckles. 1968. $3.00.
* Fluff - Mattel. (See Series II, page 198).
Growing Heidi - Remco. (See Series I, page 265). $4.00.
Growing Sally - Remco, 1968. $4.00.
* Growing Up Ginger - Mattel. 1975.
Growing Up Pepper - Ideal. Smaller Pepper head on Dodi body. $6.00.

* Growing Up Skipper - Mattel. 1974.
  Happy Hallie - Hong Kong. $2.00.
  Heidi - Remco. 1966. (See Series I, page 263). $3.00.
  Jan - Remco. 1966. (See Series I, page 263). $4.00.
* Jr. Miss - AE. Also called Marty. $2.00.
* Kid Sister - Eegee. Also called Little Sister. (See Series II, page 85). $2.00.
  Kitty Koed - Fun World. (See Series II, page 127). $4.00.
  Lassie - Hong Kong. One of International Series. $1.00.
  Libby Littlechap - Remco, 1963. $15.00.
  Lil Shopper - Hong Kong. Boxed by Toy House. $1.00.
* Little Laurie - Amsco. $2.00.
  Little Shopper - Hong Kong. $1.00.
* Little Sister - Hong Kong. $1.00.
* Lola Ballerina - Germany (Deluxe). $6.00.
  Marty - AE. Also called Jr. Miss. $2.00.
* Mary Lou - American Character. $8.00.
  Miss Lorrie - Bella Hess. 1967. (Skipper type) $2.00.
* Miss Pre-Teen - Princess Grace Doll Co. (Mego). $2.00.
  Patches - Pedigree, England. Sindy's sister. $10.00.
  Patti - Ideal. Pepper's friend. 1964. (See Series II, page 152). $5.00.
  Peggy - Plastic Molded Arts. $3.00.
  Penny Brite - Deluxe Reading, 1963. (See Series I, page 62.) $4.00.
* Penny Sweet - Perfekta. $3.00.
  Pepper - Ideal. Tammy's little sister. (See Series II, page 155). 1963. $5.00.
* Pepper, Posin' - Ideal. $5.00.
  Pete - Ideal. Also called Salty; same doll, different clothes. (Series II, page 155). $7.00.
  Poppet - Pedigree, England. Patches' friend. $8.00.
* Posin' Sandy - Hong Kong. $3.00.
* Ricky - Mattel. (See Series I, page 198).
* Sandra Sue - Richwood. $12.00.
* Sandy - Unique. $3.00.
* Sandy - Famus. $2.00.
  Scooter - Mattel. (See Series I, page 198).
* Shirley Ann - Ideal. $15.00.
* Shirley Temple - Ideal (See Series I). $25.00.
* Skipper - Mattel. (See Series I, page 198).
  Soul sister - Fun World. (See Series I, page 127). $2.00.
  Spunky - Remco, 1966. $4.00.
* Tiff - Mattel. 1972.
* Todd - Mattel, 1966. (See Series Ii, page 52).
  Twinkie - Marx, 1966. (See Series I, page 194). $6.00.

* Tutti - Mattel, 1966.
* Vanity - Marx. $2.00.

Vacious Vicky - Hong Kong. Boxed by Toy House. $1.00.

Wendykins - Madame Alexander, 1957. (See Series I, page 23). $12.00 - $35.00.

Wonder Doll - Jak Pak. $2.00.

World of Love - Hasbro: Adam - $6.00, Love - $5.00, Peace - $5.00, Soul - $5.00, Flower - $5.00, Music - $9.00. Also: Bonnie Breck - $10.00, right Guard Premiums - $12.00. (See Series I, page 133). 1971. $5.00.

## 7½" - 13": Action Figures, meant for boys.

Azark - Hamway: Dracula, Frankenstein, Wolfman, Mummy, Creature from Black Lagoon., Wild Bill Hickock, Wyatt Earp, Billy the Kid, Kung Fu, Young Kung Fu.

Deluxe Reading: Fighting Tigers, Pretty Boy, Big ears, Machine Gun Mike, Tex.

Edico: Adventurer.

Elite:*Fighting Ace.

Excel: Pocohontas, Cochise, Annie Oakley, Wild Bill Hickock, Calamity Jane, Buffalo Bill, Deadwood Dick, Belle Starr, Davy Crockett, Jesse James, Wyatt Earp, Gen. George Washington, Lt. Col. Paul Revere, Gen. Robert E. Lee, Gen. Ulysses S. Grant, Lt. Col. Theodore Roosevelt, Gen. John Pershing, Gen. Douglas MacArthur, Adm. Wm. Halsey, Gen. Joseph Stilwell, Gen. George Patton, Gen. Claire Chennault, Gen. Dwight Eisenhower.

Gabriel: Lone Ranger, Tonto, *Butch Cavendish, Dan Reed, Red Hand, Little Bear.

Gilbert: James Bond, Napoleon Solo, *Illya Kurakin, Honey West, *Moon McDare, Odd Job.

Hasbro: *Atomic Man, *GI Joe, Nurse Jane, *Defenders, Bulletman, The Invaders.

Hong Kong: Bicentennial Heros: George Washington, Patrick Henry, LaFayette, Nathan Hale, Ben Franklin, Thomas Jefferson, Daniel Boone, John Paul Jones, Paul Revere, Amigo Adventurer, Big Red (Spiegel exclusive), Sarge, Action Fighter, Action Soldier, Adventurer, Armed Forces Action Figures, Red Boy.

Ideal: Capt. Action, Batman, Superman, Phantom, Aquaman, Buck Rogers, Flash Gordon, Green Hornet, Sgt. Storm, Canyon, Spiderman, Capt. America, Lone Ranger, Tonto, Action Boy (3 outfits - Superboy, robin and Aqua Lad), Evil Kneivel.

International: Action Buddy.

Kenner: *$6 Million Dollar Man, Bionic Woman, Boy Scouts, Cub Scouts.
Kresge: *All Pro Sportsman.
Lesney of England: *Peg Leg, *Capt. Hook, Ghost of Capt. Hook.
L.J.N.: Emergency Squad (John & Roy), The Rookies (Willie, Terry, Mike, Chris, & Lt. Ryker), SWAT (Nelson, McCabe, Deacon & Jim Street), Police Girl Nurse, Highway Patrol, Forest Ranger, Mr. Action, *Double Action.
Madelman, Spain: *Mounties.
Marx: Buddy Charlie, Archie & Jughead.
Mattel: Big Jim, Josh, Jack and Jeff. *Olympic Jim, *Dr. Steel, Wolf Pack Jim, The Whip, Warpath. Com. Koenig, Prof. Bergman, Dr. Russell.
Mego: Richie, *Fighting Yank, Hombre, The Baron, Yankee Brovo (Ward's exclusive), *Capt. Action, Ward's renamed Baron, Adam & Robbie for girl trade, Joe Namath, Wyatt Earp, Sitting Bull, Davy Crockett, Cochise, Buffalo Bill Cody, Sir Lancelot, King Arthur, Ivanhoe, Friar Tuck, Will Scarlett, Little John, Captain Patch, Black Beard, Long John Silver, Jean Lafitte, Supergirl, Batgirl, Wonder Woman, Catwoman, Dorothy, Scarecrow, Tin Woodsman, Cowardly Lion, Wizard of Oz. Bad Witch, Glenda the Good Witch, Lt. Uhura, Capt. Kirk, Scotty, Dr. McCoy, Spock, Klingon, Dinah-Mite, Action Jackson, (3 versions, white, beard and black), Planet of apes: Cornelius, Zira, Dr. Zaus, Soldier Ape, Astronaut, Galen, Gen. Urko, Gen. Ursan, Peter Burke, Alan Vernon; Super Heroes: Batman, Robin, Superman, Aquaman, Capt. America, Capt. Marvel, Spiderman, Tarzan. Alter Egos: Clark Kent, Bruce Wayne, Dick Grayson & Peter Parker. Super Foes: Joker, *Riddler, Penguin, *Mr. Mxyzptlk, Green Goblin, Lizard, The Hulk, Green Arrow, Iron Man, The Falcon, Dracula, Wolfman, Mummy, Frankenstein, Dare Brothers; The Waltons: John Boy, Mary Ellen, Ma, Pa, Grandma, Grandpa; Mohammed Ali, Cher, Sonny, Cronoh, The Torch, Invisible Girl, Fantastic Four, Our Gang (6), Mighty Thor, The Thing, Muchkins, *Fonzie.
Mortoys: *Johnny Strong.
Pengo: *Action Buddy.
Reliable, Canada: Bobby Orr.
Rosko-Steele: *Johnny Hero.
Totsy: Bill Champ, Randy, Chuck.
Shindana: O.J. Simpson, *Super Agent (Slade).
Makers Unknown: British Soldier, Hessian Soldier, Continental Soldier, *Military Boy, *Big Red (Wards exclusive), Toni.

**Action Figures with molded-on clothes.**
American Character: Bonanza: *The Cartrights - Little Joe, Ben, Hoss and Adam. (Later Adam sold as an outlaw).
Marx: Aquanat, *Cowboy, Indian, Astronaut, Johnny West, Jane, Jay, Jamie, Josie, Janice, Chief, Cherokee, Princess Wildflower, *Sam Cobra, Pat Garrett, *Jed Gibson, Fighting Eagle, Daniel Boone, Gold and Silver Knights, Detective Mike Hazard, Vikings, Stoney (Soldier with same head as Buddy Charley), *General Custer.
Mattel: Matt Mason, Doug Davis, Jeff Long, Sgt. Strorm, Scorpio, Calisto, Capt. Lazer, Sea Devils, Chuck, Rick, Kreator & Zark.

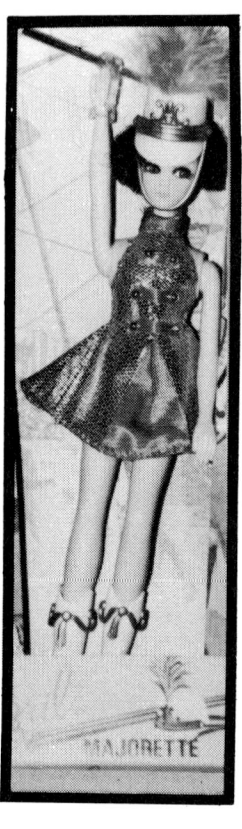

6" "APRIL MAJORETTE". Brown eyes to left. Black hair. Bending knees. Jointed right elbow. Not shown in the Dawn series booklets. MARKS: 166/H17.

6½" "CINDY JOY". Plastic and vinyl. Jointed waist. Bendable legs. Molded lashes. MARKS: M/J/MT, on head. MORT ALEXANDER LTD/MADE IN/HONG KONG, on back and box. $1.50

6" "BARBRA" by Playmate. On market 1976. Plastic with jointed waist. Bending legs. Vinyl solid arms. Brown painted eyes to side, grey eyeshadow & 3 long painted lashes below eyes. This is a Dawn doll and marked K-11A on head. 1970/Topper Corp./Hong Kong/P. on back. Pack has Topper Dawn and Mattel Rockflower clothes. Plastic case in pack: Dina/Dawn Model Agency. Courtesy Joan Asherbraner. $4.50

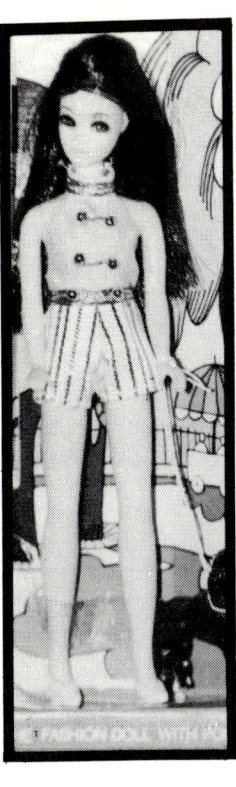

6" "DIANA". This is a "Dawn" doll by Deluxe Topper, only there is no manufacturer's information on the doll nor the box. Brown decal eyes/lashes. Brown hair. Bending knees. Black poodle. MARKS: 385/K10, on head. Courtesy Ellie Haynes. $4.00

6" "DAPHNE". An all original model in another dress that is yellow/gold. Courtesy Marie Ernst. $8.00

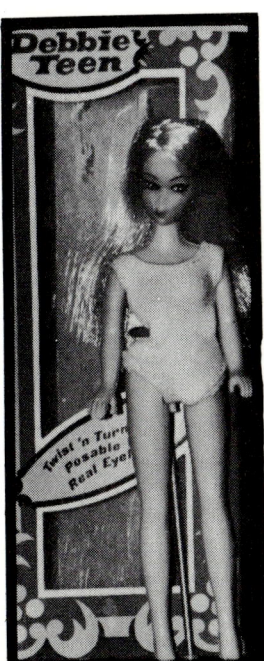

6¼" "DEBBIE TEEN". Plastic body with solid vinyl arms & legs. Vinyl head with blue eyes to side & blue shadow. Jointed waist. Top of head is almost flat. MARKS: HONG KONG, on back. No information on box. Courtesy Bev. Gardner. $2.00

7½" "DINAH-MITE". Fully jointed plastic with vinyl head. Painted brown eyes. MARKS: MEGO CORP/1972, on head. MEGO CORP./MCM LXXII/PAT. PENDING/MADE IN/HONG KONG, on back. $4.00

6" "DORABLE DOREE". Plastic & Vinyl. Jointed waist. Grow hair feature. Walker. Blue painted eyes to left. Came with fashion wardrobe. Made by Jilmar Co. MARKS: HONG KONG. Courtesy Marie Ernst. $2.00

6½" "FASHION WORLD". Plastic and vinyl. Painted eyes with very long lashes. Bendable legs. Jointed waist. Original. MARKS: HONG KONG, on back. BOX: MANUFACTURED EXCLUSIVELY FOR DANDEE DOLL MFG. CORP. $1.50

7½" "JEANIE". Plastic body with hollow plastic upper legs. Solid lower legs. Solid vinyl arms. Vinyl head with inset lashes & painted black eyes to side. Jointed waist. Orange rooted hair. High heels. MARKS: MADE IN/HONG KONG, on back. Pac: For Kresge. Courtesy Bev Gardner. $1.00

6½" "JUDY". Hollow vinyl legs with solid vinyl arms. Plastic body. Jointed waist. Wire in legs to pose them. Open/closed "ooh" type mouth. Long inset lashes. MARKS: HONG KONG, head & back. BOX: Day Fran/Dis't. by D & F Ind. Inc. Courtesy Joe Bourgious. $1.00

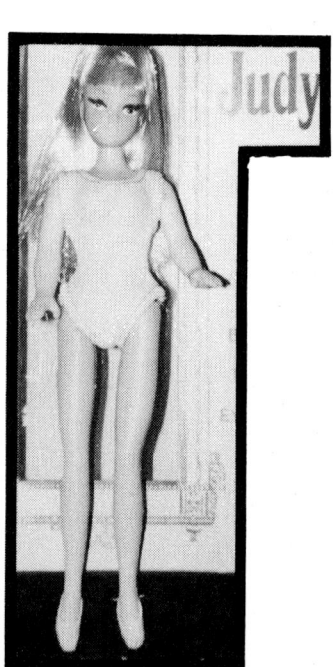

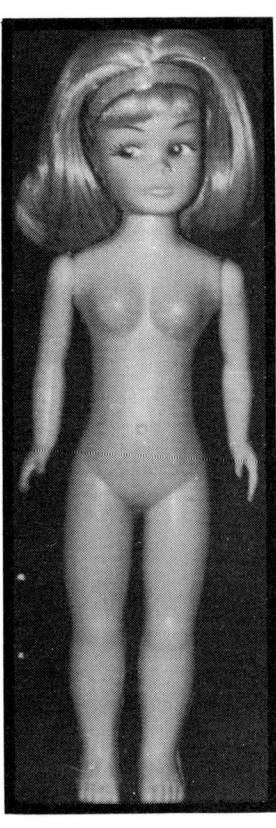

7½" "MARCIA ANN". All plastic with vinyl head. Also came with jet black hair. Head band original & permanent. This doll without head band is currently sold by Standard Doll Parts.
$3.00

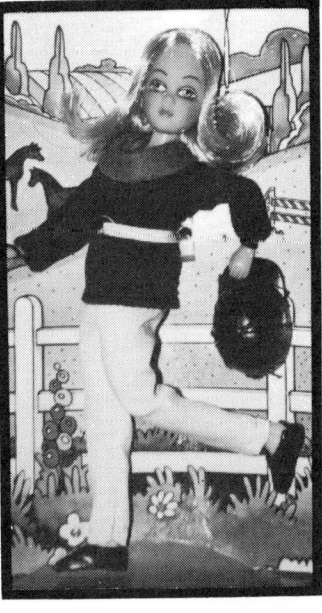

5½" "SUKY". Pocket Size Playmate. All vinyl with jointed waist and bendable limbs. Doll has extensive wardrobe and the basic doll comes as Horse Rider (Shown), Ballerina, Nurse, Shopper, Tennis Player and Skater. MARKS: LESNEY/1974/ HONG KONG, on back. LESNEY/1973, on head.
Still Available.

5½" "SUKY". Shown in the basic Ballerina outfit. Torso and legs are painted white.
Still Available.

6" "TINY TINA". All vinyl. Painted blue eyes. Wearing a Dawn dress. MARKS: HONG KONG. Made by Totsy. Courtesy Phyllis Houston. $3.00

5" "TINY TEEN-SPORT TIME". All vinyl with long inset lashes over brown with blue rim painted eyes. Original. Ice skates glued to shoes. MARKS: TINY-TEENS/U-NEEDA DOLL CO. INC. MCML XXII/MADE IN HONG KONG. Courtesy Marie Ernst. $4.00

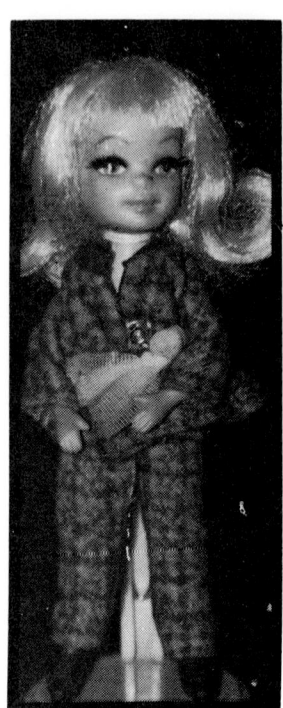

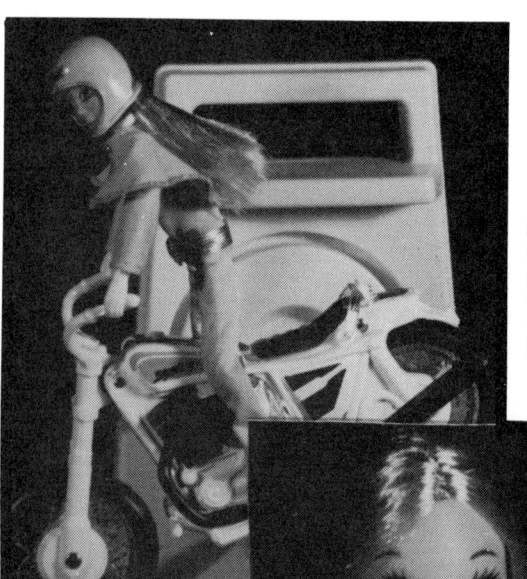

8'" "DERRY DARING". One piece wired body & limbs. Gauntlet plastic hands. Original. MARKS: 1974/IDEAL, in an oval, on head, 1974/IDEAL, in oval/HONG KONG, on back. Still Available

9" "FOREST RANGER & POLICE GIRL". Plastic with vinyl head & arms. Jointed waist. Painted blue eyes. Open/closed mouth. MARKS: LJN/1974, on head. HONG KONG, at waist. Original.
Still Available

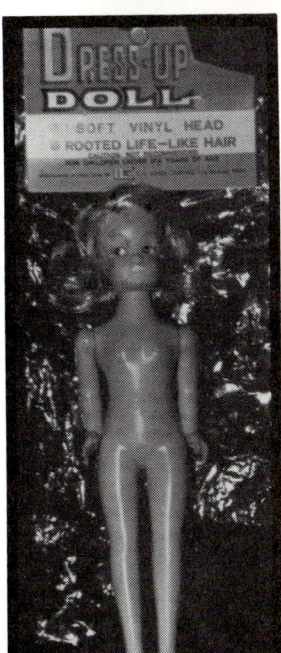

8" "DRESS UP DOLL". One piece body and legs of "soft" plastic. High heel feet. Rigid plastic arms. Vinyl head with painted blue/black eyes. Comes in shoes only. MARKS: MADE IN HONG KONG, on back. Package: MFG. IN HONG KONG FOR KRESGE CO.

8½""DRESS YOURSELF DOLL". 1968 by Grant Plastic Co. MARKS: MADE IN HONG KONG/2013.
Under $1.00

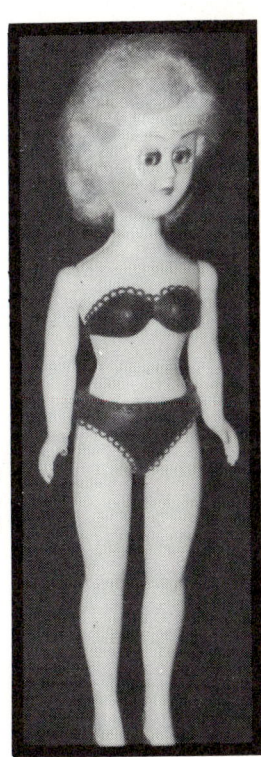

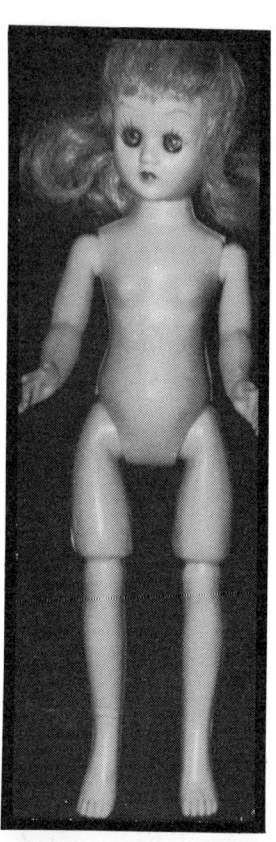

View of 8½" "HIGH HEEL TEEN" by Virga to show body. Courtesy Bessie Greeno.

8½" "HIGH HEEL TEEN", by Virga. All hard plastic with pale blue sleep eyes/molded long lashes. High heel feet. Jointed at knees. 1957. MARKS: none. Original. Courtesy Marie Ernst. $6.00

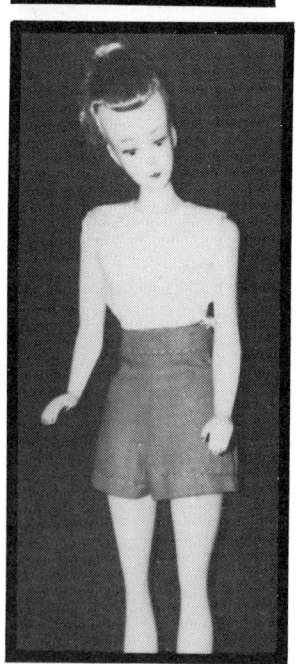

8" "GINA TEENAGE FASHION MODEL". Ponytail hairdo is set into cut out in plastic. Doll is strung. Painted blue eyes in center with blue shadow. Very high heel feet. Painted black shoes. Round holes in feet for stand. Bright red lips and nails. MARKS: MADE IN/HONG KONG, on back. Made by Allison Corp. 1960. $4.00

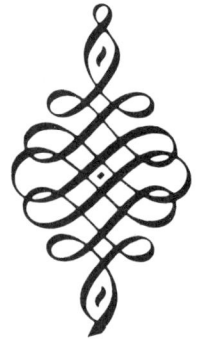

8½" "JENNY JONES". Very "dumpy" mother figure. Good quality. rigid plastic body, rest vinyl. Bending knees & elbows. Med. heel feet. Painted blue eyes straight ahead. Pale green eyeshadow. MARKS: 1973 G.M.F.G. INC./KENNER PRODS. DIV./Cinti. O. 45202/ Made in Hong Kong. $8.00

8" "JUDI". All vinyl. Rooted saran hair. Sleep eyes/molded lashes. High heels. MARKS: nine. By Belle. Courtesy Bessie Carson. $3.00

8½" "LITTLE SHOPPER". Plastic & vinyl. MARKS: HONG KONG, on back. Under $1.00

8½" "LITTLE MISS GINGER". All vinyl with jointed waist. Sleep eyes. Painted toe and fingernails. Rooted hair. MARKS: LITTLE MISS GINGER, on head. Made by Cosmopolitan. $6.00

8½" "NIKKI". Vinyl & plastic made for FW Woolworth Co. 1972. Original. MARKS: HONG KONG, on head. MADE IN HONG KONG, back. $1.50

8" "MARGARET". All soft vinyl. Adult figure. Painted red high heel shoes. Fully jointed. MARKS: JAPAN, on back. Courtesy Marie Ernst. 1.50

8" "PENNY STREET". Dark tone rubber type vinyl. Blue painted eyes to side. Black eyeliner/blue eyeshadow. Painted on high heel shoes. MARKS: JAPAN, on back. Courtesy Marie Ernst. $5.00

9" "BETTY BOOTS". Tiny Teen. Hollow plastic upper legs. Rigid plastic arms. Posable vinyl head. Large blue painted upper lashes & brown eye-shadow. MADE IN HONG KONG, on back. Pack: JAK/PAC/Milwaukee U.S.A./#402. Courtesy Marie Ernst. $2.00

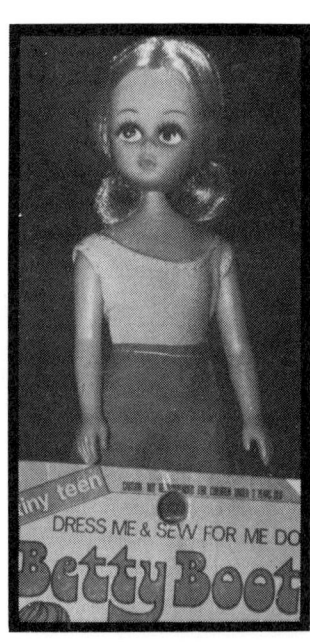

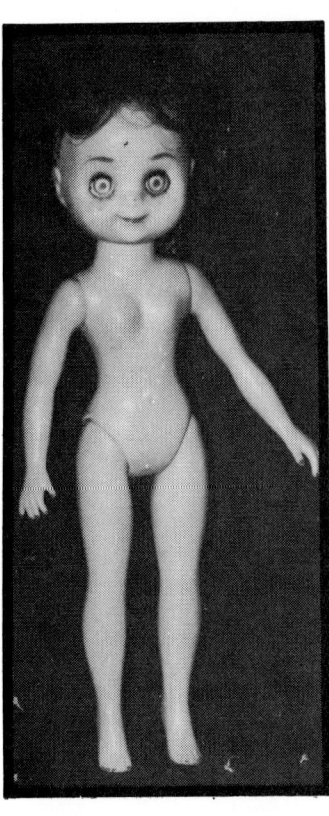
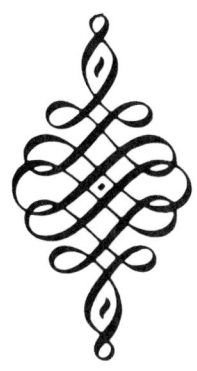
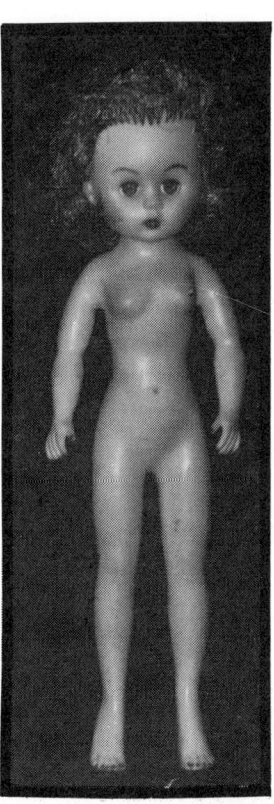
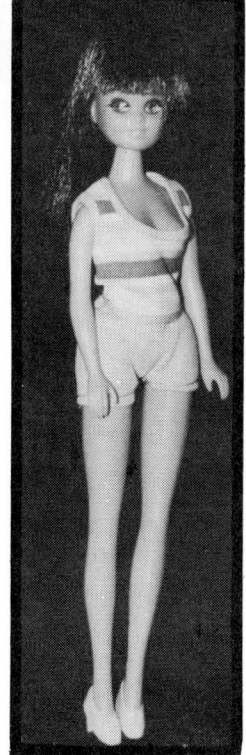

9" "BONNIE JEAN". Excellent quality vinyl. Blue sleep eyes. Feathered brows. Freckles. Smile mouth. MARKS: JAPAN, on head. $7.00

9½" "CANDI". Good quality. One piece body & legs & arms. High heels. Sleep blue eyes/molded lashes. 2nd & 3rd fingers of each hand molded together. MARKS. none. $6.00

9½" "CARLA" by Mego. Plastic body with jointed waist. Hollow plastic legs with wire for posing. Solid vinyl arms. Vinyl head. Brown/blue painted eyes with inset lashes. Brown shadow. Dimples. High heels. MARKS: HONG KONG, on head. MADE IN HONG KONG, on back. Courtesy Bev. Gardner. $2.00

9" "DOC. RUSSELL (GIRL)", Com. Koenig & Pro. Bergman of T.V. program, Space 1999. Made by Mattel. Good quality plastic with jointed knees. Vinyl arms & heads. Molded hair and painted features. MARKS: 1975/A.T.V. Licensing Ltd/Taiwan, on head. 1973/ Mattel Inc./Taiwan, lower back. Still Available

9½" "DAISY". All good quality vinyl with jointed waist & posable, bendable legs. Painted blue eyes. MARKS: MODEL TOY LTD/ HONG KONG, on lower back. Made for Gabriel. This one is dressed in red with white dots called "DOTTY". Still Available

9" "JODY". Rigid vinyl with vinyl head & limbs. Painted blue eyes. Red hair to floor. MARKS: DRESS TAG: AN OLD FASHIONED GIRL JODY/IDEAL IN OVAL. 1974/IDEAL, in oval/9-G-H/ 241, on head. 1975 IDEAL, in oval/HONG KONG, on lower back. This doll can be purchased with an old fashioned Country Store. Still Available

9" "LIZA JANE". Plastic with vinyl head. Yellow hair. Large, round blue eyes to side. Smile. Original. Flat feet. MARKS: MADE IN/HONG KONG. $1.50

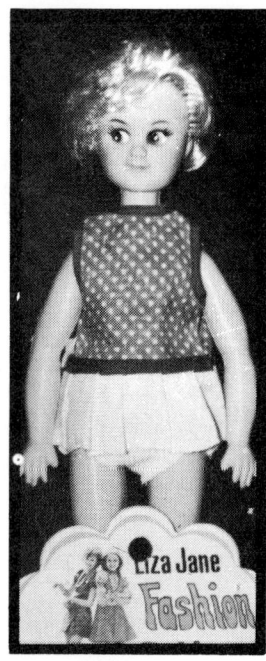

This 9" "JODY" could be purchased with an old fashioned living room setting. Also inset shows colored version.
Still Available

9" "POLICE NURSE". Plastic with vinyl arms & head. Open/closed mouth. Jointed waist. MARKS: HONG KONG, above waist. BOX: LJN TOYS LTD. 1975.
Still Available

9½" "LORRAINE" by Playmate. Late 1974 market. Her face looks almost identical to "BUSY FRANCIE" by Mattel (1972). Plastic with jointed waist. Vinyl solid arms, bending knees. Brown painted eyes. MARKS: 7-73, on head. Peggy/Von Plasty, on lower body. Courtesy Joan Asherbraner. $8.00

9½" "LORRAINE" by Playmate. Same style doll but has different hairdo (bangs) and marks are different. Number or mark on head is unreadable. Hong Kong, on back instead of the Peggy Von Plasty. Courtesy Joan Asherbraner. $8.00

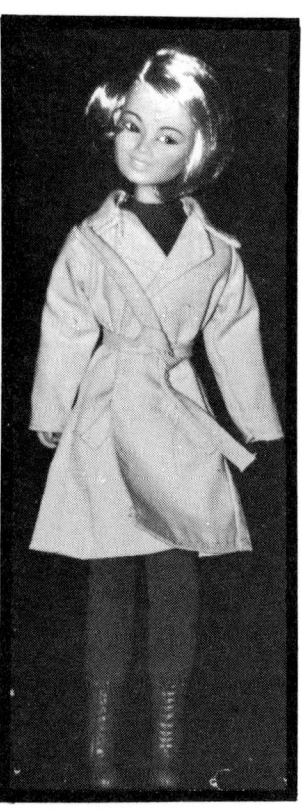

9" "POLICE WOMAN (ANGIE DICKINSON)". Rigid plastic body & arms. Posable vinyl head. Jointed elbows, wrists and posable all vinyl legs. Painted brown eyes to left. Open/closed mouth with painted teeth. Comes with 5 assignment packs. MARKS: HORSMAN DOLLS/U/L C P T/1976.
Still Available

9" "SISTER". All rigid plastic. Sleep blue eyes. Medium heel feet. MARKS: none. Made by Hasbro. 1961. $1.00

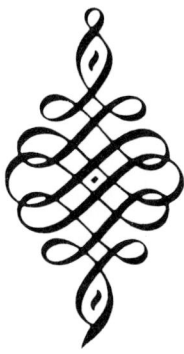

9" "VERONICA" (BLACK HAIR) & 9" "BETTY (BLONDE). All vinyl. Bending knees. Jointed waist. MARKS: MADE IN HONG KONG/MARX INC., in circle/ARCHIE ENTERPRISES/INC. 1975, on backs. Each has her name on head.
Still Available

9" "WANDA" by Shindana. First in 1973 in small red box. Box marked 1972. Came as Nurse, Ballerina, Career Girl and Stewardess. Plastic and vinyl. Bending knees. Solid vinyl arms. Inset lashes. MARKS: 1972/Shindana Toys/Hong Kong, lower back. Courtesy Joan Asherbraner.   $9.00

9" "WANDA" by Shindana. First pack box was on market early 1974 and is a larger red box. Some of the clothes (example the flowered dress) is same as one for "LORRAINE (see) and Lorraine wears the orange short set with yellow blouse. Courtesy Joan Asherbraner. $9.00

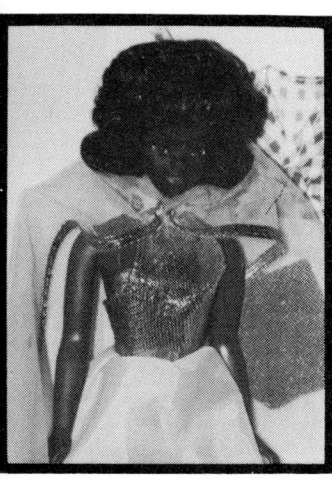

9" "WANDA" by Shindana. #2065. 1976. In a Rose colored box. Quality is still excellent. Long dress is that of career singer. Courtesy Joan Asherbraner. $9.00

10½" "ANNETTE FUNICELLO". 1961. All vinyl with dark brown rooted hair. Blue sleep eyes with molded lashes and three painted lashes at outer corners. This is the Pollyana face with dark hair. High heel feet with rather large toes and small heels. No paint on nails. MARKS: UNEEDA, on head. Courtesy Phyllis Houston. $10.00

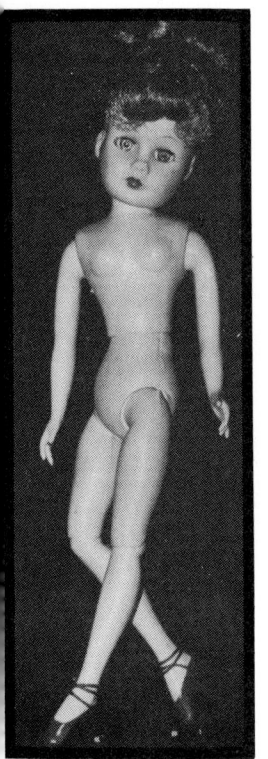

10½" "BALLERINA" by Valentine. All hard plastic with vinyl head. Jointed waist and knees. Came also with jointed elbows & wrists (Little Miss Manikin). Sleep blue eyes. MARKS: 11VW. Courtesy Jeannie Niswonger. $5.00

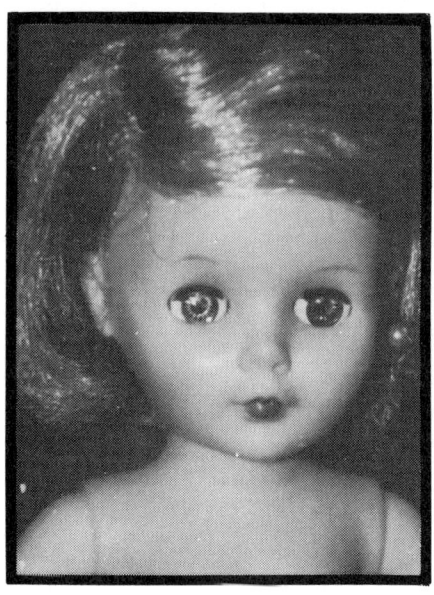

10" "BONITA". Rigid vinyl body & legs. Softer vinyl head and arms. Swivel waist. Sleep eyes/molded lashes. High heel feet. Dark fingers & toenails. Side part hairdo. Protruding upperlip. MARKS: SAYCO/DOLL/CO. See full length view with Chiltern doll. $12.00

10" "CAROL". Both are painted over vinyl, (rigid). Jointed waists and sleep eyes. MARKS: none. By Commonwealth. Courtesy Bessie Greeno. $6.00

10½" "BRIDE". Plastic & vinyl. Sleep blue eyes. High heel feet. Original. MARKS: PMA. By Plastic Molded Arts. Box just calls her Bride. $3.00

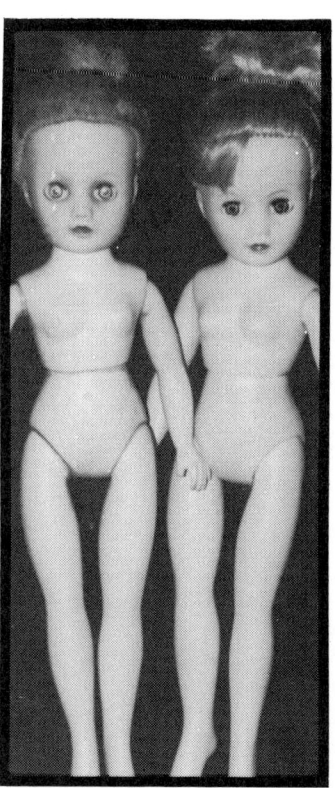

10½" "CHILTERN". All vinyl. Sleep blue eyes/hair lashes. Tiny mouths. High heel feet. Painted dark fingers & toes. Rooted black hair. MARKS: CHILTERN/MADE IN ENGLAND on head. Shown with blonde Sayco BONITA. Courtesy Sharon Hazel. $8.00

LEFT: 10" "COTY GIRL" or "MISS COTY 1958". MARKS: by R & B. RIGHT: "Miss Ritzi", who is 10½". Extra flange can be seen on both dolls at the swivel waist. MARKS: ⊗ ⓟ The larger version of Miss Ritzi may be found in the "Natural" section of Series III. $6.00

10½" "MISS COTY". All original Coty girl. All vinyl with jointed waist. Sleep blue eyes. Marked with ⊗
Tag says: Coty girl Doll by R & B Doll Co. Inc. (Arranbee). These are also marked with a ⓟ
Courtesy Jeannie Niswonger. $6.00

10½" "DEBBIE". All vinyl with swivel waist. Identical doll to "Little Miss Revlon". Made by Mayfair of Canada. MARKS: ⓟ Courtesy Mary Partridge. $5.00

Shows booklet that came with "DEBBIE" by Mayfair.

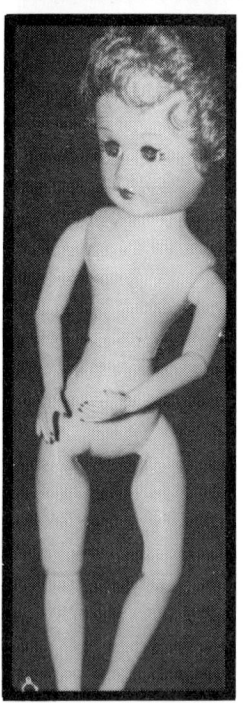

10½" "DEBBIE BALLERINA". Also "ROSEMARY BALLERINA". Hard plastic body. Vinyl head. Fully jointed including wrists. Doll is strung. Feet molded in ballerina position. MARKS: Courtesy Mary Partridge. ⓟ $4.00

10½" "FRANCINE FAIRY TALE DOLL". Came with clothes change & books of Cinderella & Alice in Wonderland. 1957. Lower body & legs are rigid vinyl. Rest vinyl with jointed waist. High heels. Nails painted red. Rooted hair. Sleep eyes with molded lashes. MARKS: none. Also used Ⓟ marked dolls. Courtesy Phyllis Houston.   $6.00

10½" "FRANCINE", as "CINDERELLA". All vinyl. Jointed waist. High heels. Long dark hair. Original costume that is black over yellow. MARKS: Ⓟ Courtesy Renie Culp.

10" "JAN". All vinyl. 1958 in original box and clothes. MARKS: VOGUE DOLL.   $15.00

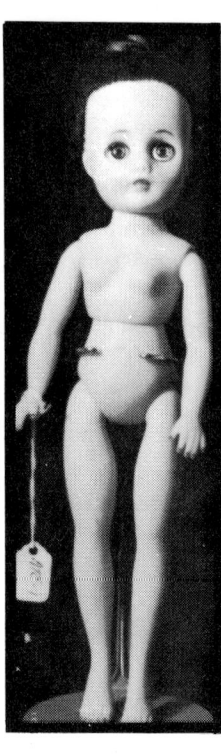

10" "JENNY". All good quality vinyl. Swivel waist. Rooted dark hair in ponytail. Almost round sleep blue eyes with molded lashes. High heel feet. painted toe and fingernails. MARKS: ATC/MADE IN JAPAN. 1956. Courtesy Phillis Houston. $6.00

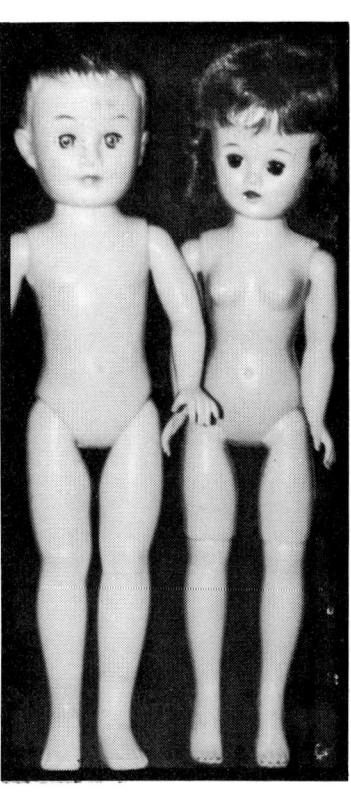

10" "JEFF & JILL", by Vogue Dolls. Jeff is all vinyl and Jill is hard plastic. Refer to Vol. 1 & 2 for full description. $15.00

"JILL". All vinyl with very pale mouth that gave her the nickname "The pink lipstick Jill". 1962. Courtesy Phyllis Houston.

Copy of "LITTLE MISS REVLON". MARKED: 27/ PLAYTHING, on head. Called "LAURIE" - 1958. Courtesy Phillis Houston.

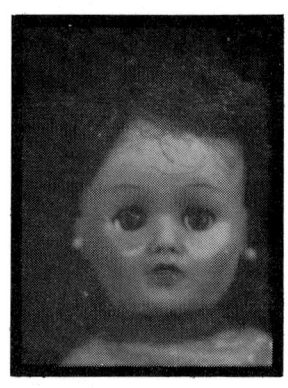

10" "JUDY". One piece body and limbs of rigid vinyl. Toe and fingernails are red. High heel feet. Rooted hair, sleep blue eyes with molded lashes. Eyebrows set high on forehead. Three painted lashes at outer corners of eyes. MARKS: ⊗
Coutesy Phyllis Houston. $5.00

10½" "LITTLE MISS MARIE". Made for Woolworths. All vinyl (hollow, not stuffed) with high heel feet, red toenails. One piece body and limbs. Rooted hair, sleep eyes with molded eyelashes and painted lashes below. Molding of seat is with dimples at end of each branch: ϒ   MARKS: none. Courtesy Phyllis Houston. $6.00

10½" "KAY". Excellent quality rigid vinyl. Walker, head doesn't turn. Jointed waist & knees. High heel feet. Sleep blue eyes/molded lashes with painted lashes under eyes. Open/closed mouth with protruding upper lip. MARKS: OH/EEGEE. Courtesy Marge Meisinger. $15.00

10½" "LITTLE MISS REVLON". All vinyl with jointed waist. Sleep blue eyes. An original outfit which includes bra and girdle. MARKS: IDEAL TOY CORP/VT-10½. 1957. $14.00

10½" "MAXI GIRL". Plastic body & legs. Vinyl arms & head. Feet peg into plastic music box. Jointed shoulders & neck only. MARKS: none. Courtesy Marie Ernst. $6.00

10½" "MISS GINGER". All vinyl with jointed waist. High heel feet. Sleep blue eyes/molded lashes. MARKS: GINGER, on head. Paper purse: Miss Ginger. TAGGED dress. Courtesy Bessie Carson. $7.00

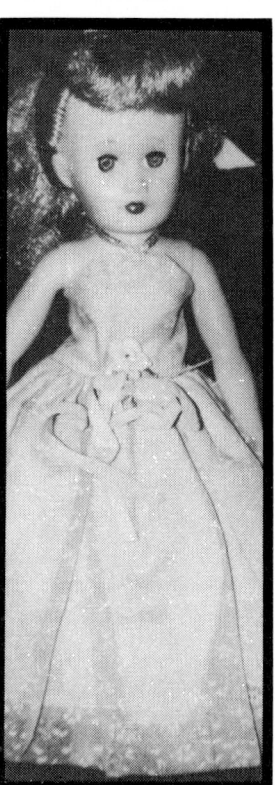

10" "MISS GIGI" (Perreau). All vinyl with jointed waist. Sleep blue eyes. Original. MARKS: none. Made by A & H Doll Mfg. Corp. Had 12 outfits, plus bride dress. Courtesy Bessie Carson. $12.00

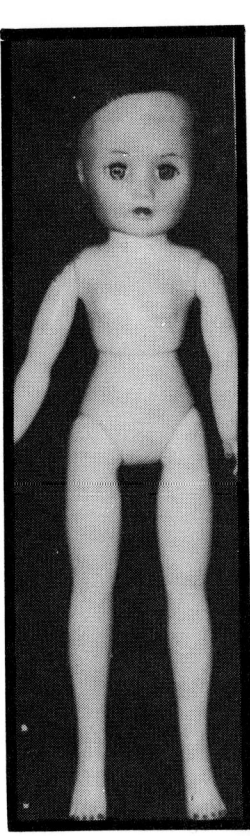

10" "MISS NANCY ANN". All vinyl. Swivel waist. High heel feet. Sleep blue eyes. MARKS: NANCY ANN, on head. Courtesy Bessie Greeno. $6.00

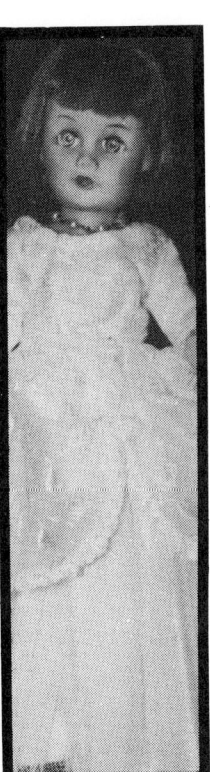

10½" "MISS RITZI". All vinyl. Jointed waist. Sleep blue eyes. High heel feet. 1959. Original Bride dress. MARKS: ⊗. Made by the Natural Doll Co. $6.00

LEFT: 10" All vinyl. Can see where waist is joined so it does not swivel. Pink hair was called Pink Fairy, blue hair, Blue Fairy, and was also Tiny Teen in 1957. MARKS: UNEEDA.
RIGHT: 10" "MISS TEENA". Jointed waist. Walker but head does not turn. 1961. MARKS: HORSMAN.
Blue Fairy $4.00
Tiny Teen $5.00

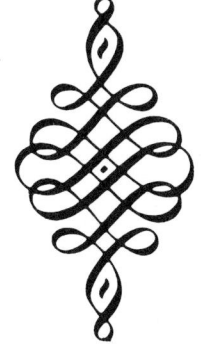

10¼" "MISS VICKI". Plastic body, arms & legs. Vinyl head. Back of feet molded very thin. High heels. Sleep blue eyes/molded lashes. Poorly rooted hair. MARKS: none. By Elite. Courtesy Sharon Hazel. $1.50

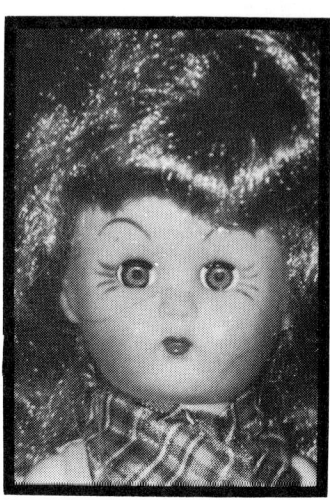

10½" "MISSY". All vinyl. Four long painted lashes. High heel feet. MARKS: PMA. By Plastic Molded Arts. Courtesy Marge Meisinger. $1.50

LEFT: 10" "PENNY" by Flagg. All rigid vinyl, softer vinyl head. Hair rooted tightly around head for upsweep. Sleep eyes/molded lashes. Swivel waist. High heels. MARKS: none. Shown with Uneeda's Blue Fairy. Courtesy Sharon Hazel. $12.00

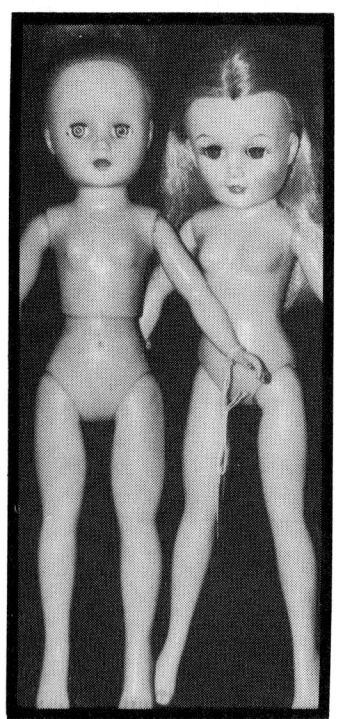

10½" "POLLYANNA". All vinyl. Sleep blue eyes. High heel feet. MARKS: UNEEDA, on head. original. Courtesy Marge Meisinger. $20.00

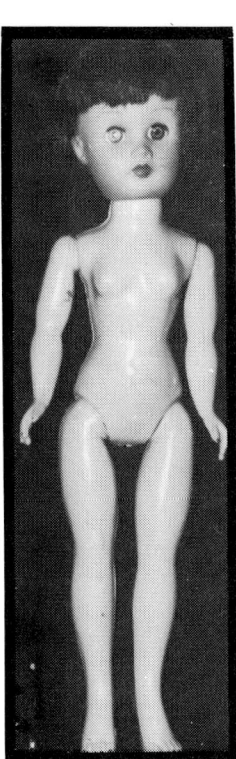

10½" "ROSEMARY". 1958. All hard plastic with vinyl head. Walker, head turns. MARKS: ⓟ made by the Rosemary Doll Co.   $5.00

10" "SHERRY". One piece stuffed vinyl with vinyl head. Vinyl arms. High heels. Sleep blue eyes. MARKS: O-H/EEGEE. Courtesy Bessie Greeno.   $4.00

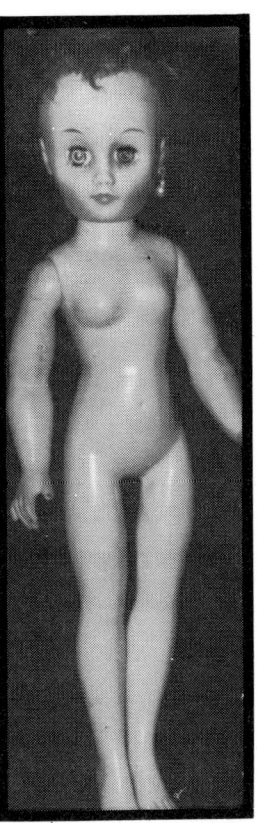

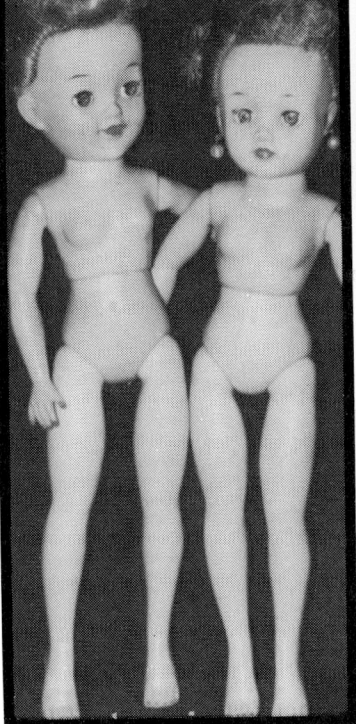

LEFT: 10½" "TEENAGE SHIRLEY TEMPLE". Open/closed smile mouth. Same body as Little Miss Revlon. MARKS: none, except 10½R under right arm. RIGHT: Little Miss Revlon. MARKS: IDEAL DOLL/VT-10½ and 10½R under right arm. Courtesy Bessie Greeno.   $15.00

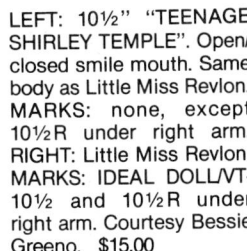

10½" "SUZETTE". All vinyl. Sleep blue eyes. MARKS: UNEEDA, on head. Original box. $5.00

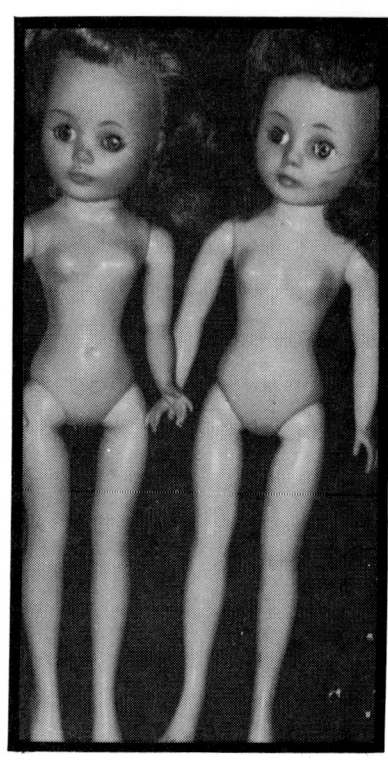

10" "TONI'S". LEFT: hard plastic arms, legs & body. Vinyl head. Sleep blue eyes. RIGHT: All rigid vinyl with softer vinyl head. Sleep blue eyes. MARKS: AMER. CHAR. 1958. Courtesy Bessie Greeno. $25.00

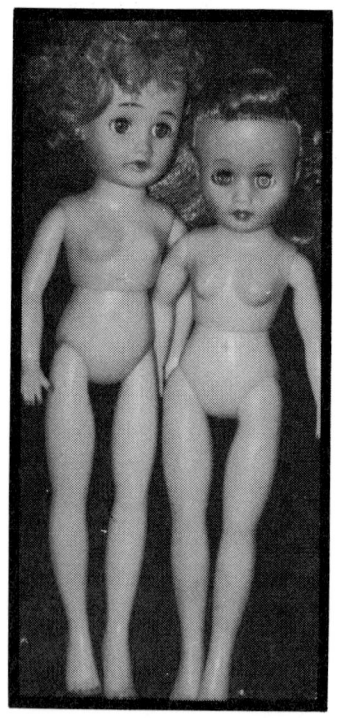

LEFT: 10" "WENDY". Pinker top body. Swivel waist. Sleep eyes/molded lashes. Swivel waist. High heel feet. MARKS: ATC/JAPAN. ATC/MADE IN JAPAN, on backs. Courtesy Sharon Hazel. $3.00

11½" "ACTION GIRL". Made in England. Same body as Dollikin by Uneeda. Courtesy Marie Ernst. $22.00

Close up of "ACTION GIRL" of England: "DOLLI-KIN" by Uneeda. $22.00

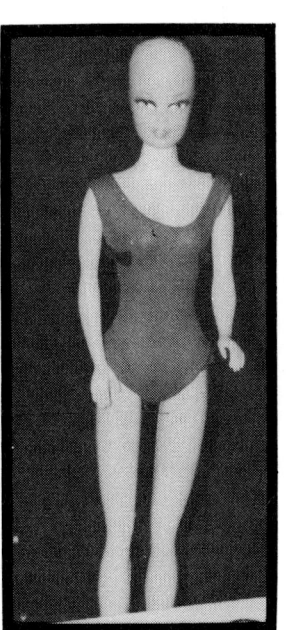

11" "ALICE". Plastic with vinyl head. Open/closed mouth. Small molded lashes. High heels. Takes wigs. Original suit. MARKS: HONG KONG. Courtesy Marie Ernst. $2.00

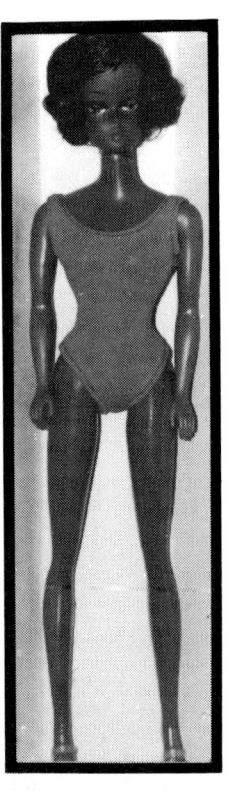

11½" "ALINE". Plastic body. Vinyl hollow "posable" legs. Painted features with heavy molded lashes. Eyes in center looking down. Small ball jointed waist. Basic blue suit. MARKS: HONG KONG, on back. Made by the NANCY ANN STORYBOOK DOLLS. $9.00

11" "ALOHA ALICE". Plastic with vinyl arms & head. Posable head. Black brows, lids and eyes. Floss type rooted dark brown hair. MARKS: MADE IN/Hong Kong, on back. HONG KONG on head. $5.00

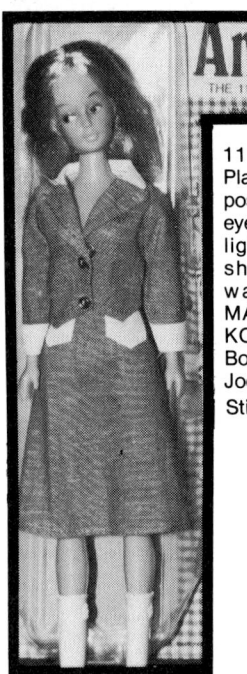

11½" "ANITA". Plastic with vinyl, posable head. Blue eyes to side with light green eyeshadow. Jointed waist. MARKS: MADE IN HONG KONG, on back. Box: GIG. Courtesy Joe Bourgious.
Still Available

11½" "ANITA". Plastic with rigid plastic arms. Jointed waist. Vinyl head with blue eyes to side. Green eyeshadow. Pale pink lips. MARKS: MADE IN/HONG KONG, on back. No package information. Courtesy Bev. Garnder.
Still Available

11½" "BABE". Sold at World's Fair 1964 as Marie Anntonette. Heavy molded eyelids and special heavy painted brows. Cut out scalp with inset human hair. All good quality rigid plastic. Painted on high heel shoes, red nails & molded on daisy earrings. Sold from French Pavillion. This is a special doll from the Lilli (W. Germany) mold and made in Hong Kong by Fab-U-Lu- Ltd. (Faber-Luft, Ltd.). $125.00 up

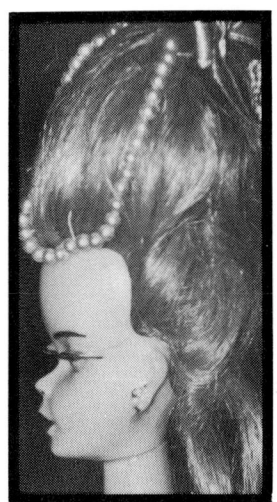

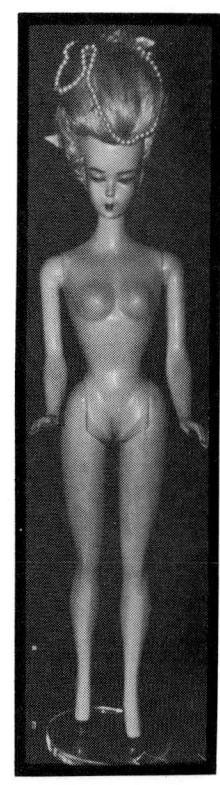

11" "BABETTE". Plastic with solid vinyl arms. Vinyl head with black eyeliner, black painted eyes and inset lashes. High heel feet with very short toes. Bright pink lips. Sharp defined nose. MARKS: HONG KONG, on head & back. No information on box. Courtesy Bev. Gardner. $4.00

11½" "BALLERINA NITA". All hard plastic. Walker, head turns. Jointed knees. High heel feet. Sleep blue eyes. Holes in feet to set on top of music box. MARKS: PAT'S PEND., on back. Made by Roberta. $6.00

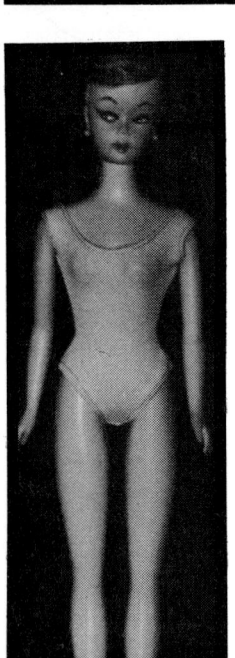

11½" "BARBARA JO". Plastic with solid vinyl arms. Vinyl head flanged over neck. Narrow black painted eyes to side. Molded lids & peaked black brows. Orange-red lips. MARKS: AE, on head. Made by New Dolly Toy Co. 1965. Courtesy Bev. Gardner. $4.00

11" "BETTY". Plastic body & legs. Good quality vinyl arms & head. Painted blue eyes/molded lashes. Sold with boyfriend Bob through Aldens. 1962. $4.00

11½" "BETSY TEEN". Suntan. Plastic hollow upper legs. Jointed waist with ball end seated into lower torso. Solid vinyl arms. Blue painted eyes to side with three painted lashes at sides, plus inset lashes. Hot pink lips. Ward's exclusive. MARKS: MADE IN/HONG KONG. No maker information on package. Bangs pulled to side into the ponytail. Courtesy Bev. Gardner. $4.00

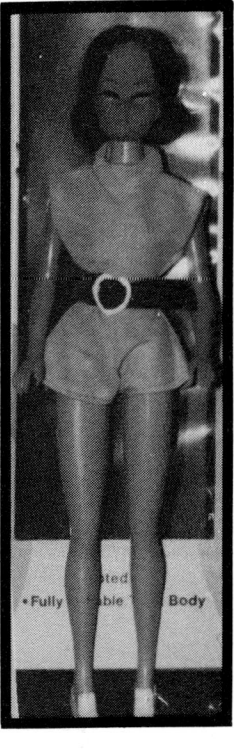

11½" "BLACK BOUTIQUE FASHION. Plastic & vinyl. BLUE painted eyes. Made by Peggy Ann Doll Clothes Inc. MARKS: none. Courtesy Marie Ernst. Still Available

11½" "CHARLY". A new girl in town. Blue/green painted eyes with long painted lashes above & below eyes. Plastic with vinyl arms & head. Jointed waist. MARKS: Hong Kong, on head, and same upside down on back. Made by Durham. Courtesy Joe Bougious. Still Available

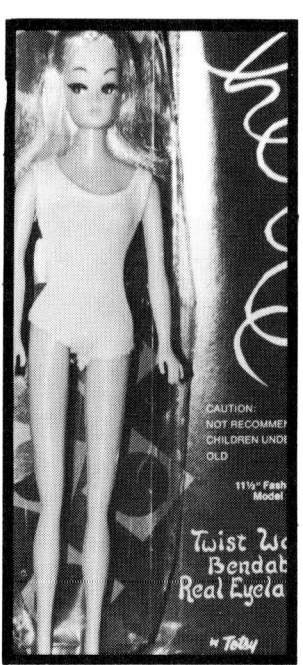

11½" "CHERIE". Boyfriend is Chuck. Hollow plastic upper legs and arms. High heels with two bumps on front of tiny feet. Vinyl head with black brows, eyes to side and heavy molded lids. Inset lashes. Posable head. MARKS: HONG KONG, on head. MADE IN HONG KONG, on back. PAC: BY TOTSY. Courtesy Bev. Gardner. $4.00

11½" "COAST TO COAST DOLL". Very pale blue eyes with pin point pupils. Grow hair feature controlled by turning left arm counter-clockwise. Straight legs. Jointed waist. MARKS: ⌐⌐ on back. Courtesy Phyllis Houston. $8.00

Different "COAST TO COAST" doll with railroad car mark on back. Jointed elbows but hair retraction is still controlled by arm movement. Courtesy Louise Ceglia. $8.00

11½" "DEAR JUDY". Plastic & vinyl. Green eyes & eyeshadow. Red/brown hair. High heels. MARKS: MADE IN/HONG KONG, on back. 1969. Courtesy Marie Ernst. $4.00

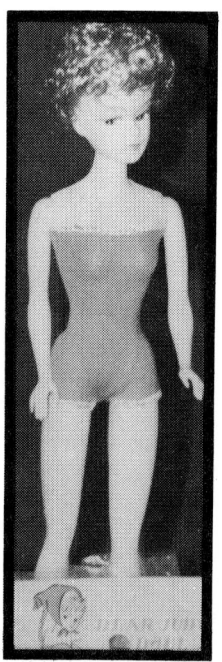

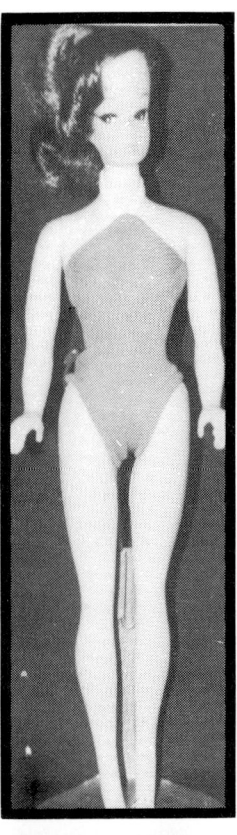

11½" "DEBBIE". Plastic with vinyl head. Jointed waist. high heels. Pale blue painted eyes. Made by the Valentine Co. MARKS: V, on head. $5.00

11½" "DEBBIE DRAKE". 1963. Plastic with vinyl head. Has extra joints, white rooted hair and black painted eyes. Black brows and molded lids. MARKS: none. Box: Valentine Dolls. Courtesy Bev. Gardner. $10.00

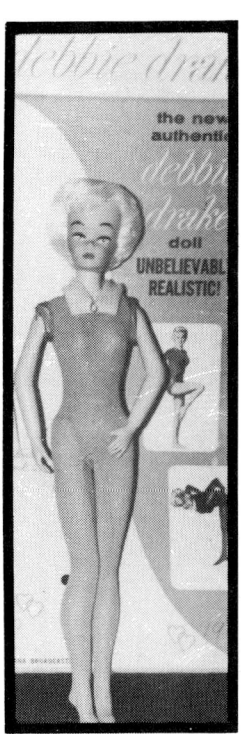

11½" "DEBBIE POSE". Same as Debbie Drake. Blonde with brown brows, eyes and heavy lids. Dark red lips. High heels. MARKS: none. By Valentine. Courtesy Bev. Gardner. $8.00

11" "DOLL CRAFT DOLL". Plastic with solid vinyl arms. Med. heel feet. Vinyl head with painted blue eyes to center. Brow/black liner. Painted lashes under only. MARKS: MADE IN/ HONG KONG, on back. Courtesy Bev. Gardner. $2.00

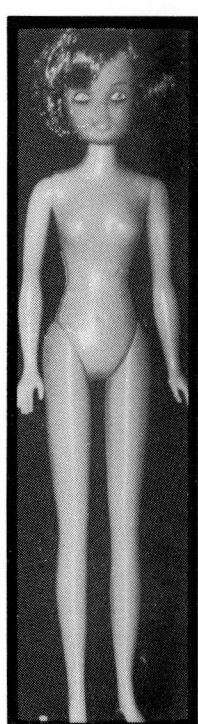

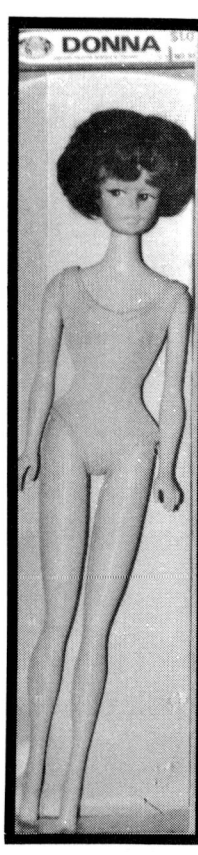

11½" "DONNA". Plastic and vinyl. Painted blue eyes with blue eyeshadow. Pink suit. MARKS: MADE IN/HONG KONG. BOX: ACTION/CHESWICK, Pa. Courtesy Marie Ernst. $2.00

11" "FASHION TEEN". Plastic with vinyl head. Rooted blonde hair in original set. Long eyes with white pupils, molded lashes and heavy black makeup. Tiny feet. Neck ends in a round ball over a posable base. MARKS: HONG KONG, on head. MADE IN/HONG KONG, On back. Courtesy Phyllis Houston. $3.00

12" "GINA TEENAGE FASHION MODEL". Plastic & vinyl. Molded on high heel shoes. Holes in bottom. Curl is glued down. Ponytail is folded and taped. Fully strung. Also came in 6" size. Made in 1960 by Allison Corp. Courtesy Phyllis Houston. $8.00

11½" "GIGI". Plastic with vinyl head. Deep purple rooted hair. Head seated into neck. Very little toe detail. Black brows, Black eyes/molded lids & heavy black liner. Red lips. MARKS: PL, on head. Natural Doll Co. Courtesy Bev. Gardner. $4.00

11½" "GIRL DOLL". Mate to "Boy" doll. Plastic hollow legs. Solid vinyl arms. Ball jointed waist. High heel feet with one molded bump over toe area. Vinyl head with blue eyes straight ahead. Single line brown liner. No lashes. Wide open/closed mouth with painted upper teeth. MARKS: NONE. Courtesy Bev. Gardner.

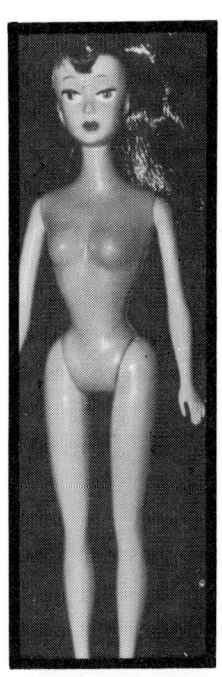

11¼" "GLORIA". Hollow plastic legs. Vinyl arms & head. Blue painted eyes with black liner. Red lips. MARKS: JAPAN, on head & lower back. Courtesy Bev. Gardner. $1.50

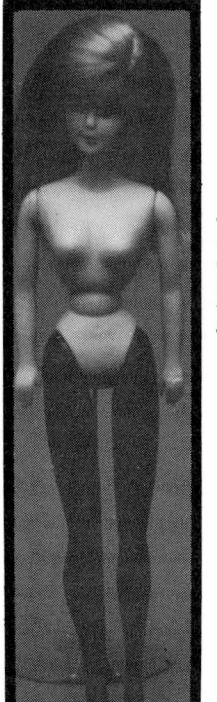

11" "GO GO GAIL". Black plastic legs with molded net. High heels. Jointed waist. Vinyl arms & head. Green painted eyes. Green eyeshadow. No molded lids. Courtesy Joan Amundsen. $8.00

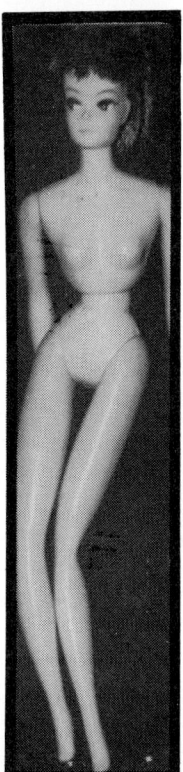

11½" "GROOVEY GIRL". Reddish/brown hair. Black eyes with white highlights. Plastic & vinyl. MARKS: PEGGY ANN DOLL CLOTHES INC / SPRINGFIELD, MASS/MADE IN HONG KONG. $2.00

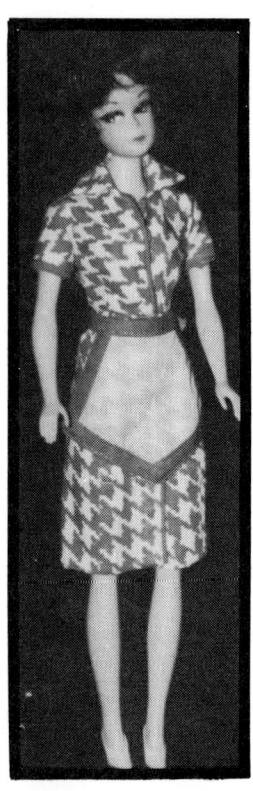

11½" "HOWARD JOHNSON GIRL". Plastic body & legs. Vinyl head & arms. Posable head. Black painted eyes/ Molded Lids. Black brows. MARKS: HONG KONG, on head. MADE IN/HONG KONG, on back. Courtesy Bev. Gardner. $9.00

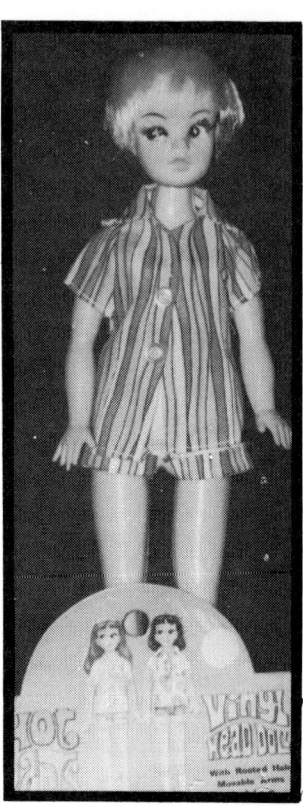

11" "HOT PANTS". Plastic & vinyl (head). Painted eyes with inset lashes. Original. Came with this short as well as longer hair. MARKS: HONG KONG on back. $1.00

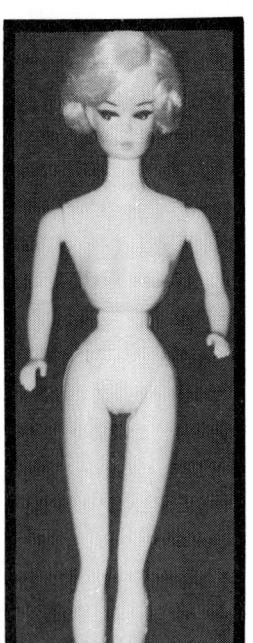

11½" "LAURIE LEE". Original hair style. Plastic & vinyl. Pale pink mouth. Black eyes to side. MARKS: HONG KONG, on lower back. Made by Ross Doll co. $2.00

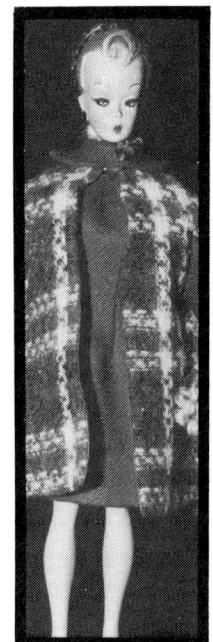

11½" "LILLI". Made in West Germany 1957 & 1958. Inset hair in cut out scalp. "Ohh" style mouth. Molded on earrings. All rigid plastic. Holes in bottom of feet for stand. Painted on high heel shoes. Courtesy Sarah Sink.
$1.00 and up

11" "LINDA". (German). Hollow upper, plastic legs & solid vinyl arms. Vinyl head with large painted aqua eyes with brown shadow and lashes painted up & down. Ears are molded beautifully and are very natural. Jointed waist. Neck fits into body. Small high heel feet. MARKS: none. BOX: Linda/Ges. Gesch Unter 744391. Made in Hong Kong for Super Market Services Corp. Dunmore, Pa. 18512. Courtesy Bev. Gardner. $6.00

11½" "LIZ". Plastic with vinyl head. Rooted yellow hair. Heavy molded lids (black) with downcast black painted eyes. High heels. Original. Sold through Safeway Stores. MARKS: MADE IN/HONG KONG, on doll. On package: No. 1822P/MADE IN HONG KONG/ FOR LOUIS GREENBERG & SONS, INC./NEW YORK, N.Y. 10010. $1.50

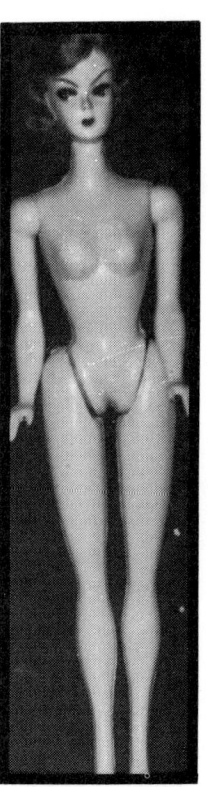

11" "LINNETTE". All rigid plastic. Red mohair wig. Head strung with arms. Painted on earrings. Bright blue eyeshadow. Dark red lips. Black long eyebrows. MARKS: HONG KONG, on back. Made for Australia. $4.00

11½" "LIZA JANE". Plastic with vinyl head. Jointed waist. Black rooted hair. Blue/black painted eyes. Indent over top of foot to hold shoe straps in. MARKS: HONG KONG, 2 across shoulder. Two bumps and an oval indentation area in center back. Courtesy Marie Ernst. $1.50

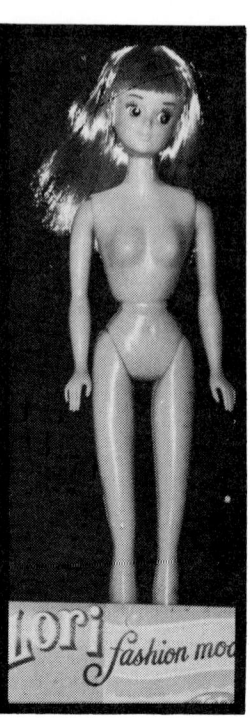

11½" "LORI FASHION MODEL". Plastic with two bumps molded over the toe area. High heel feet. Ball jointed waist. Plastic arms. Vinyl head with very large, to the side, blue painted eyes. Painted lashes over eyes only. Very pale pink lips. MARKS: HONG KONG, on head. MADE IN/HONG KONG, on back. Package: By Totsy/Holyoke, Mass. Courtesy Bev. Gardner. $3.00

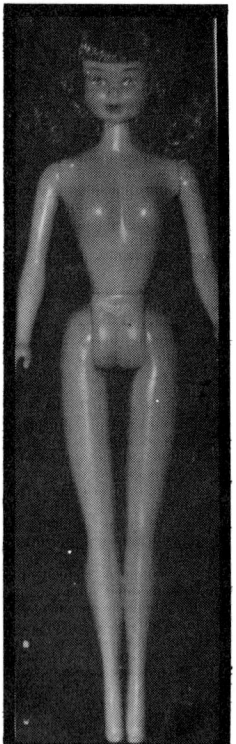

11½" "MADDIE MOD". (Original). Hollow plastic legs. Jointed waist. Solid vinyl arms. Vinyl head with blue painted eyes to center. Blue shadow & no lashes. Closed smile mouth. High heel feet. MARKS: 1968/Princess Grace Doll/Hong Kong (Mego). Courtesy Bev. Gardner. $4.00

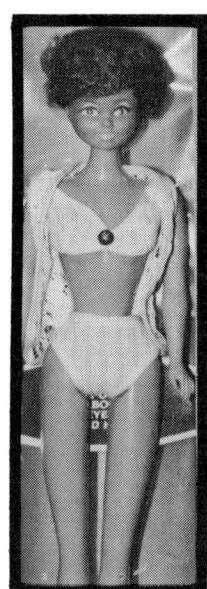

11½" "BLACK MADDIE MOD". Blue eyeshadow/lashes. Made by Mego in 1970. Courtesy Marie Ernst. $4.00

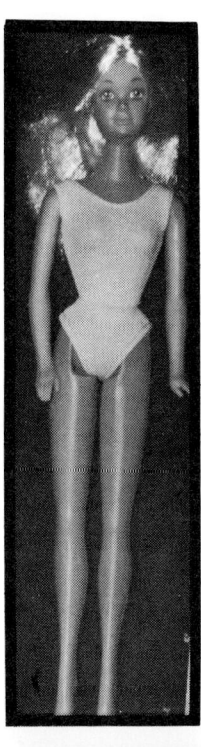

11½" "WARD'S MADDIE MOD". Plastic legs and body. Vinyl arms & head. Jointed waist. Posable head. Blue painted eyes with white and red dot highlights. MARKS: MEGO CORP. MCMLXX/HONG KONG, on back. 1974 MEGO CORP., on head. Sold through Montgomery Wards 1975. Courtesy Marie Ernst. $5.00

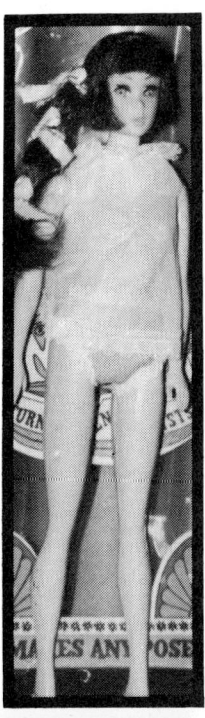

11½" "MARCIE MOD." Blue/green painted eyes with lashes. Also came with blonde hair. MARKS: HONG KONG, on back. BOX: A & H DOLL/ 1970. Courtesy Marie Ernst. $2.00

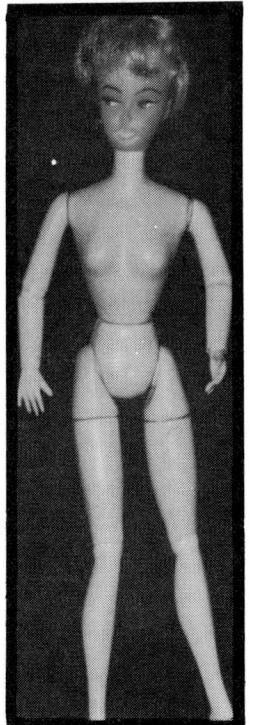

11½" "MARLENE." Plastic with vinyl head. Extra joints at elbows, wrists, waist, knees. MARKS: MADE IN HONG KONG/MARX TOYS, in circle. LOUIS MARX & CO. INC/MCMLXIV. Courtesy Marie Ernst. $4.00

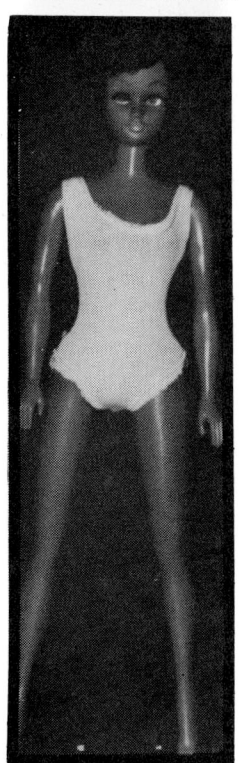

11½" "BLACK MAXI MOD". Brown painted eyes. Original. MARKS: M & S/SHILLMAN, on head. MADE IN/HONG KONG, on back. 1973. Courtesy Bev. Gardner. $3.00

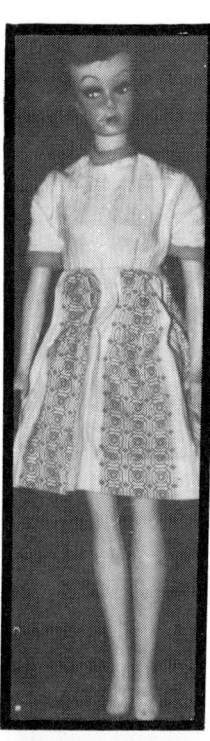

11½" "MARZIE". Plastic & vinyl. Heavy arched brows. Black eyeshadow. Molded eyelids. High heels. Made by Allied Doll Co. 1964. MARKS: none. $1.00

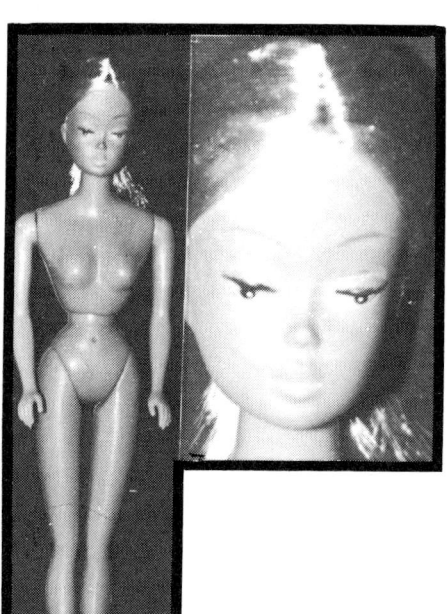

11¼" "MELISSA". 1972. Suntan rigid plastic with jointed waist. Vinyl head with "drooping" heavy molded lids. Aqua painted eyes and shadow. MARKS: Hong Kong, on upper torso. By Mortoys (Mort Alexander ltd.). Courtesy Bev. Gardner. $1.50

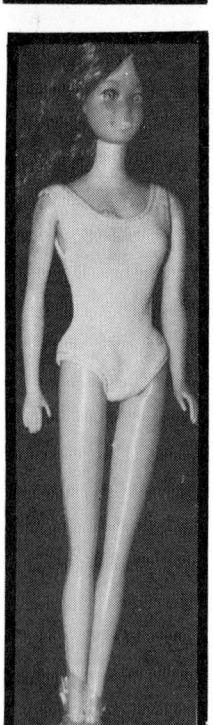

11¼" "MELISSA". 1973. Hollow plastic legs (upper) with plastic body. Jointed waist (flush jointed) solid vinyl arms. Vinyl head with large round blue eyes with blue eyeshadow. Open/closed mouth. Painted upper lashes. MARKS: 11A/D/HONG KONG, on head. By Mortoys (Mort Alexander). Courtesy Bev. Gardner. $1.50

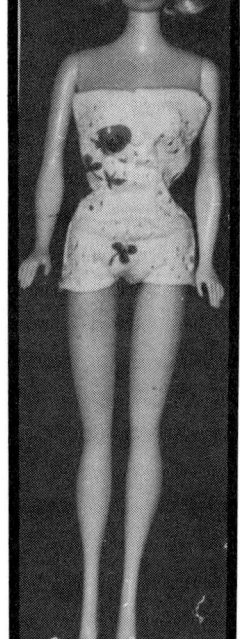

11½" "MILLIE". Plastic with vinyl head. Freckles. Painted blue eyes to front. Black liner. No molded lids. MARKS: EVERGREEN/BRITISH COLONY/OF HONG KONG. Courtesy Bev. Gardner. $2.00

11½" "MISS BABETTE". Plastic & vinyl. Came with & without cut bangs. MARKS: E.G., on head and also EEGEE/61, on head. Courtesy Marie Ernst. $6.00

11½" "MISS CAMAY". Plastic & vinyl with pierced ears. High heels. Painted white eyes. Pin point black pupils. Courtesy Marie Ernst. $5.00

11½" "MISS FANCY". Pierced ears. Black eyeshadow. Molded lids. Frosted brown hair. MARKS:JAPAN. Made by A.T.C. $4.00

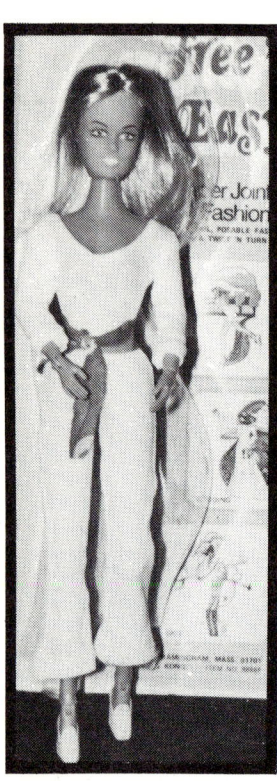

11½" "MISS FREE'N EASY". Full action figure. Middle three fingers of each hand molded together. MARKS: HONG KONG, on head & lower back. BOX: Zayre Corp. Courtesy Joe Bourgious.
Still Available

11½" "MISS FREE 'N EASY". Action jointed plastic with vinyl head. Painted features and rooted hair. MARKS: HONG KONG, on back. Petite by LJN, on bubble package. Still Available

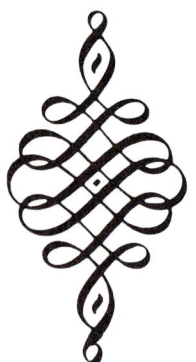

11½" "MISS PETITE FASHION". Small high heel feet. Plastic and vinyl. Original. MARKS: none. PACKAGE: Head of clown/L.J.N. TOYS LTD.
Still Available

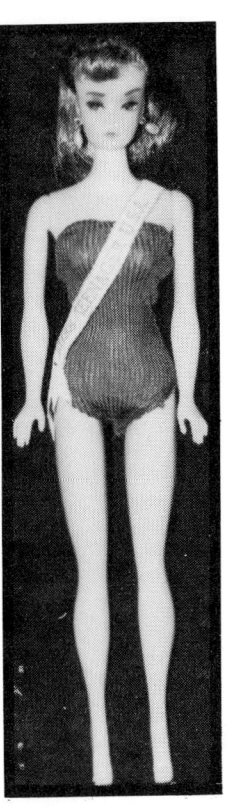

11½" "MISS TEENAGER U.S.A.". All plastic with vinyl head. Ponytail hairdo. Blue painted eyes with black rims and molded lids. Brown brows. Pierced ears. Red suit. Bare high heel feet with molded on straps for shoes. MARKS: EVERGREEN/BRITISH COLONY/OF HONG KONG/1011½, on back. Courtesy Bev. Gardner. $6.00

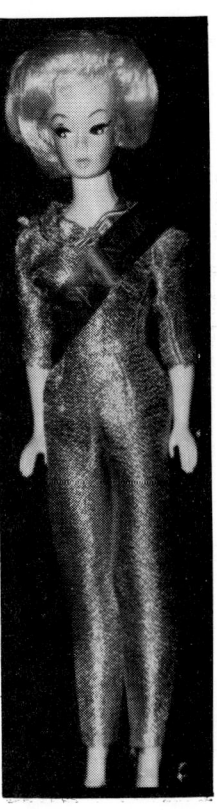

11½" "MISS SPACE NEEDLE", for Seattle's Worlds Fair. Came with pale blue, pink or green hair. Brown brows. Black painted eyes with molded lids and long extended line from corner of eyes. MARKS: U, on head. Courtesy Bev. Gardner. $9.00

11½" "MISS WORLD FASHION". Rigid plastic with vinyl head. Jointed elbows, waist, knees & ankles. Original. Comes with stand. Made by Jilmar. MARKS: MADE IN/HONG KONG. Courtesy Marie Ernst. $6.00

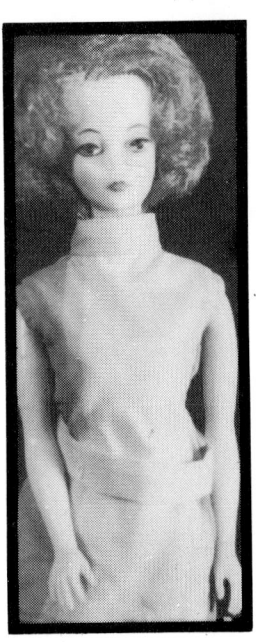

11½" "MITZIE". Plastic and vinyl with rooted reddish hair. Painted eyes with heavy black on lids and molded lashes. Tiny mouth. MARKS: RELIABLE/CANADA, on back. Courtesy Phyllis Houston. $4.00

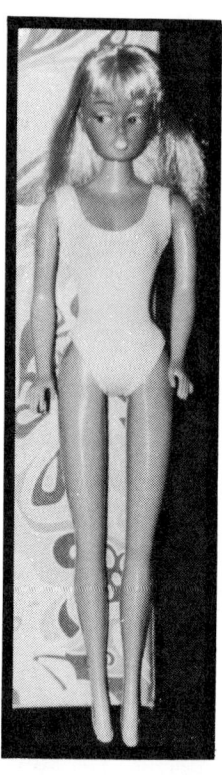

11½" "MODERN MISS". All plastic with vinyl head. Jointed waist. Painted blue eyes with blue shadow. Suntan. MARKS: MADE IN/HONG KONG, on back. By Edico. Courtesy Joe Bourgious. $2.00

11" "MOLLY". Plastic with solid vinyl arms. "Little girl" face. Blue painted eyes to side. Painted lashes at sides only. Open/closed mouth. MARKS: 4/My Toy Co. Inc./1966. Courtesy Bev. Gardner. $2.00

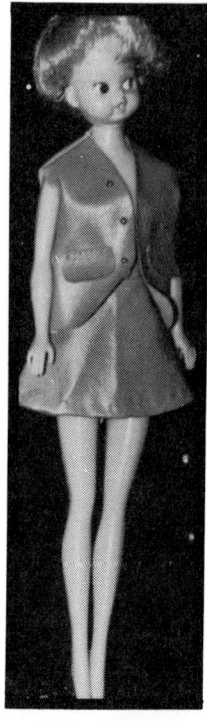

11" "MS. TONI". Kit made by WALCO. Foam with vinyl arms and head attached to plastic base with name. Clothes are pinned and glued on. Still Available

11" "NINA BALLERINA". Excellent quality. Plastic body & legs. Left one molded in one piece. Right jointed at knee. Leotards & ballerina slippers molded on. Hole in left foot to fit stand. Solid vinyl arms. Vinyl head with large painted eyes to side. Waist is not jointed. MARKS: Figure of two children/ TOMY/1975/HONG KONG. Courtesy Bev. Gardner. Still Available

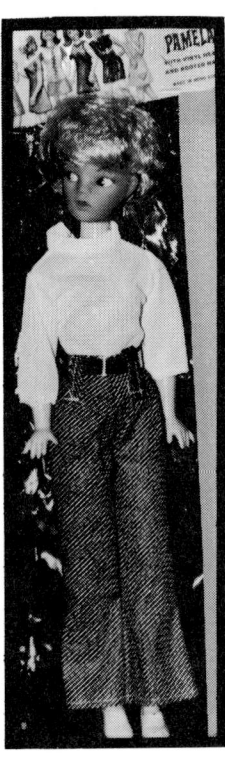

11½" "PAMELA". Plastic with vinyl head. Flat feet. Painted blue eyes with 3 long painted lashes. Blonde rooted hair. Original. MARKS: MADE IN/HONG KONG, on back. Package: ITEM NO. 751-212/DAN BRECHNER & CO. INC. $2.00

11½" "PAULINE". Plastic with vinyl head. Black eyes with blue whites. Hair lashes, extend way beyond end of eyes. High heel feet. Jointed waist. Pale pink legs. Original. Holes in heels of shoes (only) for stand. MARKS: MADE IN HONG KONG. $2.00

11½" "PETITE FASHION". Plastic hollow legs. Solid vinyl arms. Vinyl posable head. Side part hair. Blue painted eyes straight ahead. Painted lashes over and under eyes, at outer corners. Pink lips with very small upper lip. MARKS: HONG KONG, on head. MADE IN/HONG KONG, on back. Courtesy Bev. Gardner. Still Available

67

11½" "POLLY TURNER". Plastic with vinyl head. Jointed waist. Rooted hair is part white and part brunette. Top of head turns to change hair color. MARKS: MADE IN/HONG KONG, on back. Sold from Aldens, 1975. Courtesy Marie Ernst. Still Available

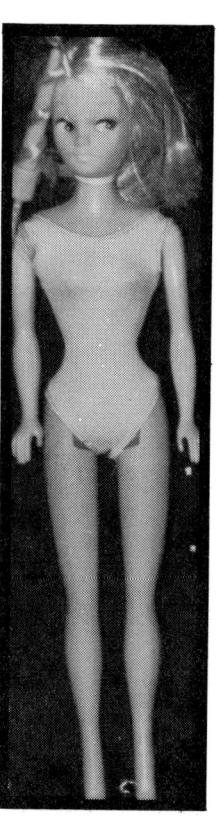

11½" "POLLY POS'N CURL". Made for Spiegel. MARKS: MADE IN/HONG KONG, on back. Courtesy Marie Ernst. $4.00

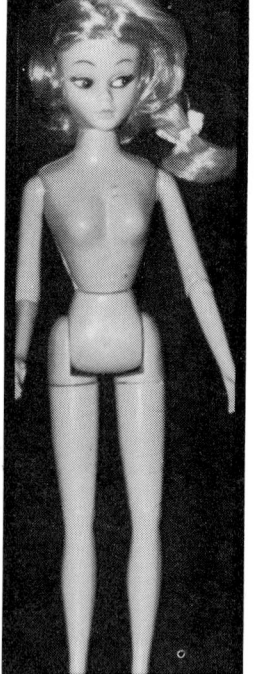

11½" "POSIN' POLLY." Plastic with vinyl head. Grow hair feature. Extra joints at elbow, waist, below hips & ankles. MARKS: HONG KONG, Lower back. $5.00

11½" "POP'S GIRL". Plastic with vinyl head. Jointed waist. Blue painted eyes to side. MARKS: MADE IN/HONG KONG, on back. Courtesy Marie Ernst. $2.00

11½" "POSEY", the Jewel Tea Co. doll. Body by Marx & head by Valentine. Plastic with vinyl head. Black brows and liner on molded lids. Blue painted eyes to front. Jointed waist, elbows, wrists and above knees. $6.00

11" "PRETTY MISS". Plastic with vinyl head. Unjointed waist. Black heavy molded lids. Green liner. Ridge across fat feet to hold shoes on. MARKS: HONG KONG, at shoulder. Courtesy Marie Ernst. $1.50

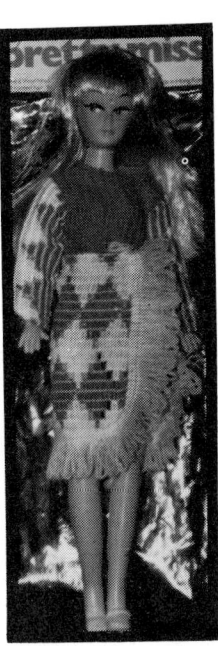

11½" "RAINBOW FASHION DOLL". Suntan. Plastic with jointed waist. Solid vinyl arms. Vinyl head with painted blue eyes to side/molded lids and black liner. Rose/pink lips. Very curly "shag" hair style. MARKS: HONG KONG, on back. No information on package. Courtesy Bev. Gardner. $4.00

11½" "SCARLET". All vinyl Painted eyes. Slight heels. MARKS: 12-40, high on head. Ⓝ JAPAN, on back. DRESS TAG: Ⓝ SCARLET JAPAN. Courtesy Mary Partridge. $10.00

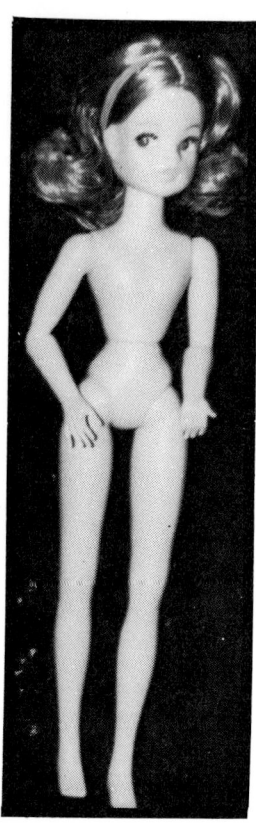

11¼" "SINDY". All excellent quality vinyl with body of the rigid vinyl. Posable head. All but head strung. Bending knees. Lower arms fit onto upper arms like gloves. Open/closed mouth. Painted blue eyes/heavy lashes. MARKS: 033055X, on head. MADE IN HONG KONG, on back. BOX: MADE & PACKED IN GREAT BRITAIN BY ROVEX/INDUSTRIES LTD. SOME PARTS/MADE IN HONG KONG. Sindy's friends were: VICKI, PATCH & POPPET. Bracelet in box says SINDY. End of box reads: FASHION DOLL BY PEDIGREE. Courtesy Shirley Peustzer.
Still Available

11" "NEW ACTIVE SINDY". Same body construction except the ankles can be bent to pose. MARKS: 033055, on head. MADE IN/HONG KONG, lower back. Made by Pedigree, England and sold exclusively through FOA Schwartz, 1975. Still Available

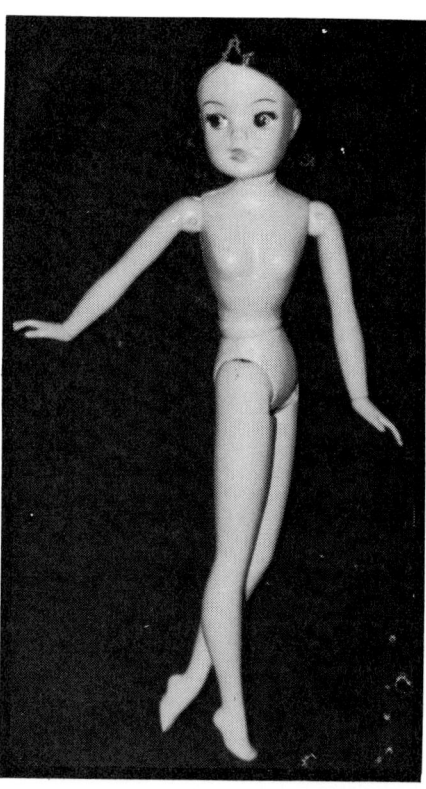

## FREE - a new friend for Sindy - June - Save Sindy Heart Tokens

June, is Sindy's new friend and you can get her FREE if you collect Sindy Heart Tokens. You only need 24 Hearts and June is yours.

She will come to you ready to be dressed with any of Patch's wonderful outfits which are shown in the new Sindy catalogue.

To start your collection of Hearts there are two already on this card so you only need 22 more.

The date of closure of this offer will be announced on two occasions in the Sindy Club page of June and School Friend and The Daily Express or successors thereof.

The offer only applies in the United Kingdom.

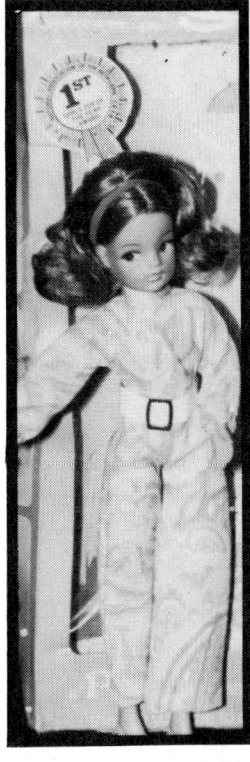

Shows slip that was in Sindy Box.

Shows "SINDY" in original box.

11" "SINDY" in her original FAO Schwartz costume. Still Available

11½" "STILJOY". Heavy plastic body with vinyl limbs and head. Snapping posable legs. Posable arms. Painted blue eyes. Also has plastic figurine (paperdoll style) in box. MARKS: SEBINO/MADE ITALY, on head. 006, on back. Still Available

11½" "SUSIE". Soft plastic with vinyl head. Jointed waist. Blue painted eyes/green eyeshadow. MARKS: MADE IN HONG KONG, on back. Manufacturer unknown. $1.50

11½" "SUZETTE". Marked N.F., on head. UNEEDA/DOLL CO/INC. in a circle/1962 on back. Original clothes, gold 1 pc. slacks & shoes. Deep rose top with gold collar & cuffs. White top stitching. To above elbows cut out in sleeves. Wide gold belt.

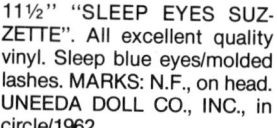

11½" "SLEEP EYES SUZZETTE". All excellent quality vinyl. Sleep blue eyes/molded lashes. MARKS: N.F., on head. UNEEDA DOLL CO., INC., in circle/1962.

"SUZETTE". Delicate, dainty molded hair by Uneeda. Sleep eyes. Also released as "ANNETTE LEE" and "WENDY WARD". Courtesy Louise Ceglia.

11½" "SUZETTE". 1975. #1890. Plastic with solid vinyl arms. Vinyl head with large round brown painted eyes straight ahead. Jointed waist. Good quality rooted hair. Very high heeled feet. Better than average quality. Currently S & H Green Stamp premium. MARKS: MADE IN/ HONG KONG, on back. Package: B I & D/Brothers Import & Development Ltd. Courtesy Bev. Gardner. $1.50

11½" "SUNKISS-ED BOUTIQUE". Soft plastic and vinyl. Open/closed mouth. Jointed waist. Suntan. MARKS: HONG KONG, on back. Made by Peggy Ann Doll Clothes Inc. Still Available

11' "SWINGIN' SALLY". Plastic with vinyl head. Rooted red/brown hair. Painted blue eyes. Green eyeshadow. Pale Pink lips. Jointed waist. High heel feet. Posable head. Original. MARKS: MADE IN HONG KONG, on back. $1.50

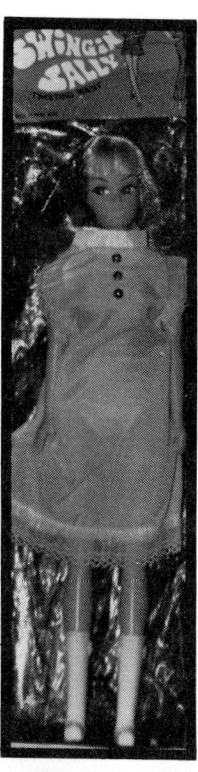

11" "SWINGIN' SALLY". Plastic with vinyl head. Jointed waist. Very sharp, upturned nose. Black painted eyes with green liner. MARKS: HONG KONG, on shoulders. Courtesy Marie Ernst. $1.50

11½" "TINA". Dark suntan. Hollow plastic legs. Vinyl arms & head. Jointed waist. Large blue decal eyes/inset lashes and painted black upper lashes. Side parted hair. MARKS: MADE IN/HONG KONG. Courtesy Joe Bourgious. $1.50

11½" "TINA MARIE". Made for Woolworths. Plastic with vinyl head. High heels. MARKS: U, on head. $3.00

11½" "TRENDI". Plastic & vinyl. Jointed waist. Small high heel feet with toe detail. Blue painted eyes/lashes. Blue eyeshadow. MARKS: MADE IN/HONG KONG, on back. $1.50

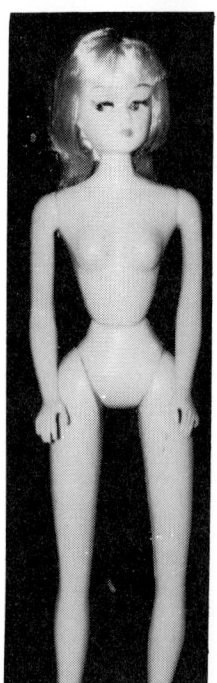

11¾" "VALERIE" also "MOD JUDY". Very cheap plastic with hollow plastic ponytail that swivels 360°. Black eyes with white pupils. Heavy black around eyes. Molded hair is light brown. High heel feet. MARKS: MADE IN/HONG KONG. Courtesy Phyllis Houston. $1.00

11½" "VALARIE". Plastic with vinyl head & arms. High heels. Molded lashes. MARKS: DANTEX/MADE IN HONG KONG, on back. HONG KONG, on head. Courtesy Marie Ernst. $2.00

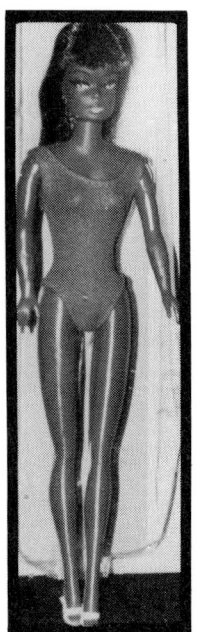

11½" "WIGGY" by Larimie. Also called Mod Judy & Janie. Plastic with vinyl head. Head seated into neck. Takes wigs & has molded painted brown hair. Single bump on foot to hold on shoes. Black painted eyes to side/molded lids and heavy black eyeliner. MARKS: none. $1.50

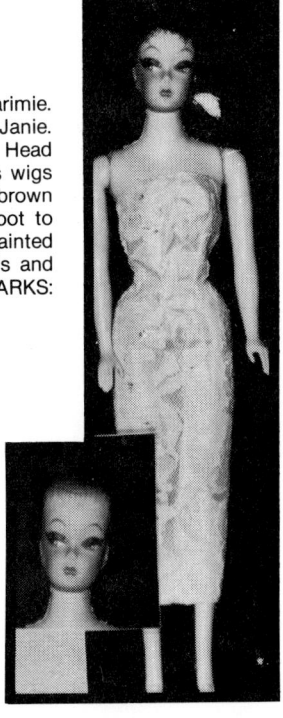

11½" "TWISTEE". Plastic hollow upper legs. Jointed waist. Solid rough vinyl arms. Black eyes/molded lids. Pink lips. High heel feet. MARKS: HONG KONG, on head. Pack: by Totsy/Holyoke, Mass. Courtesy Bev. Gardner. $2.00

12" "AMERICAN AIRLINES". Made by American Character Dolls. Pale pink lips. Blue eyes to side/no lashes. Light brown eyeshadow. High heels. Same doll as Mary Make Up. MARKS: none. $8.00

12" "CALICO LASS". Plastic & vinyl. Painted blue eyes. Premium doll offered by Kellogs. MARKS: UNIQUE, on head. $4.00

12¼" "CHER". Plastic body with jointed waist. Plastic hands with jointed wrists and very long nails. Rest is vinyl. Painted eyes with inset long lashes. Black hair to knees. Bendable elbows and knees. MARKS: 3906/AF, high on head. MEGO CORP/1975, lower on head. Still Available

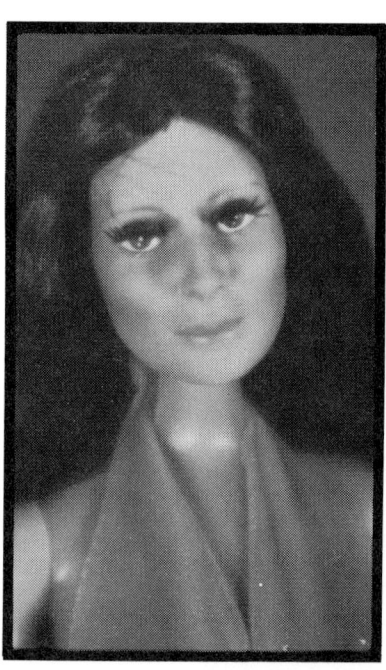

11½" "DUSTY". Bending knees and jointed wrists. Came in several different sports outfits. MARKS: 50/G.M.F.G.I., on head. 1974 GMFGI KENNER PRODS./CINN. OHIO 45202/"DUSTY"/MADE IN HONG KONG, on back. Still Available

11½" "ELLIE MAE CLAMPET". Plastic & vinyl. Same as the Kellog's 1964, Calico Lass. MARKS: UNIQUE, on head. $4.00

12" "FULLERETTE". Dark red brown hair. Painted blue eyes. 3 painted lashes at sides. Posable head. Hand molded to hold plastic bag. High heels. MARKS: HONG KONG, on back. Distributed by The Fuller Brush Co. Courtesy Bev. Gardner. $10.00

11½" "FIFI". All plastic. Mohair wig. Doll is strung. Red molded lashes. Sleep blue eyes. Long fingers. Socket head. High heels. From Australia. MARKS: MADE IN HONG KONG/BRITISH EMPIRE/No. 6120 and UP in circle. Courtesy Marie Ernst. $3.00

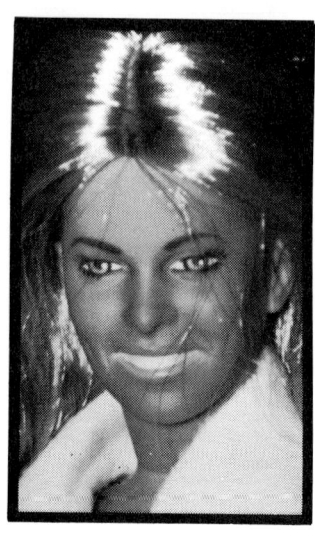

12" "JAIME SOMMERS", The Bionic Woman. Full action figure with "roll up" vinyl oversleeve on right arm. Head turns to make clicking noise, hole in right ear. MARKS: General Mills Fun Group/Inc. 1976 by it's div. Kenner Products Cincinnati/Ohio 45202. Cat. No. 65800./Character: (blank)/Universal City Studios/Inc. 1974/All rights reserved. Still Available

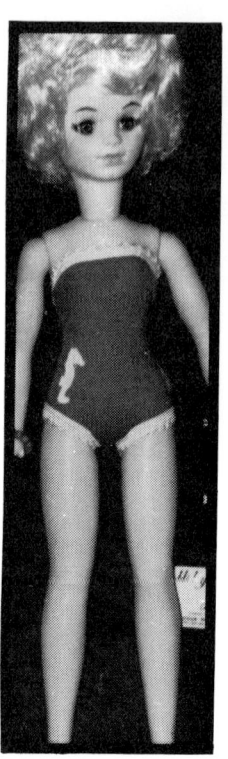

12" "JAN" #9230. Sleep blue eyes. MARKS: VOGUE, on head. Courtesy Marge Meisinger. $15.00

12" "LISA JEAN". Plastic body. Jointed waist. Vinyl legs. Bending knees. Med. heels. Solid vinyl arms. Vinyl posable head. Inset blue eyes/lashes. Open/closed mouth. Has little girl face on teen body. MARKS: 17201/-Furga, in square/italy & Furga emblem. Courtesy Marie Ernst. $9.00

12" "JENNIFER". Plastic with vinyl arms & head. Blue sleep eyes/molded lashes. "Fat" legs with small feet. MARKS: Jennifer on head. Some are unmarked. Made by C.G. Morgan Co. $6.00

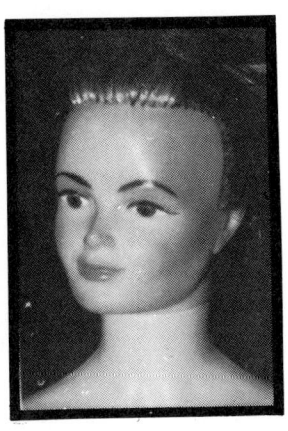

13¾" "LISA LITTLECHAP". Plastic and vinyl. White streak in hair. MARKS: LISA/Littlechap/Remco Industries/1963. B92, left leg. B95 right leg. $20.00

"JUDY LITTLECHAP". Plastic & vinyl. MARKS: Judy Littlechap/Remco Industries/1963. $15.00

12½" "MIA". All hard plastic with flirty, sleep blue eyes. Flat feet & small busts. An original outfit. Made in Italy by Bonomi. 1961. Courtesy Jeannie Niswonger. $12.00

12" "MERLENA". Plastic with vinyl head. Green eyeshadow. An original "snake-skin" dress. MARKS: SHARING/3001. $6.00

11½" "MISS CHELSEA". Plastic hollow legs & arms. Thin at heels with good toe detail. Rigid plastic head. Sleep blue eyes/molded lashes. Dark red lips. Glued on mohair. MARKS: HONG KONG, on head & back. Made in Canada. Courtesy Bev. Gardner. $4.00

12" "MISTY" (Tammy's best friend) Original. MARKS: 1965/IDEAL TOY CORP./W-12-3. $2.00

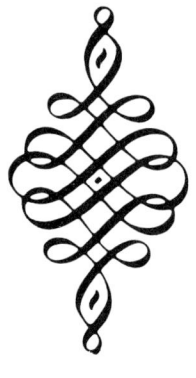

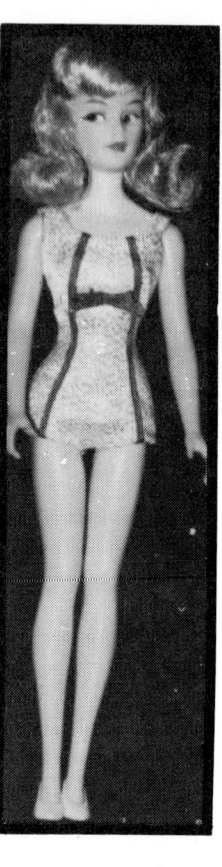

12" "POSIN' MISTY". Original. Box is made like a phone booth. MARKS: 1965/IDEAL TOY CORP/W-12-3. $2.00

11½" "MITZI". All rigid plastic. Sleep amber eyes/ molded lashes. Mohair in one long braid. One piece body & legs. Jointed neck & shoulders. MARKS: RELIABLE/MADE IN CANADA, on back. 550-5, on flattened place inside each arm. $5.00

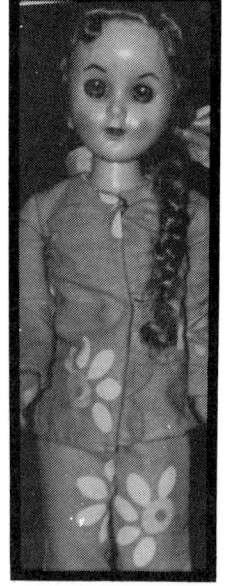

11½" "PATTY DUKE" with eyes to the left rather than to the right. Same body & legs that are flexible vinyl. Mouth is longer, more pink than red and not as full. MARKS: HORSMAN DOLLS INC./66121 and an 8 in a circle. Courtesy Phyllis Houston. $16.00

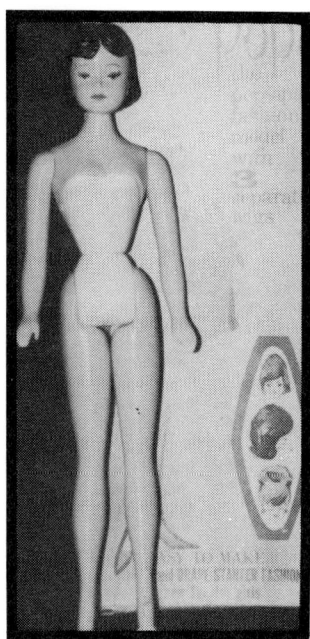

12" "POPI". All plastic with 3 vinyl wigs. Light tan painted eyes. Two painted lashes. Pops apart. Wigs are Blonde, red & black. MARKS: none on doll. BOX: AMERICAN DOLL & TOY. Courtesy Virginia Jones. $9.00

Shows "POPI" in parts.

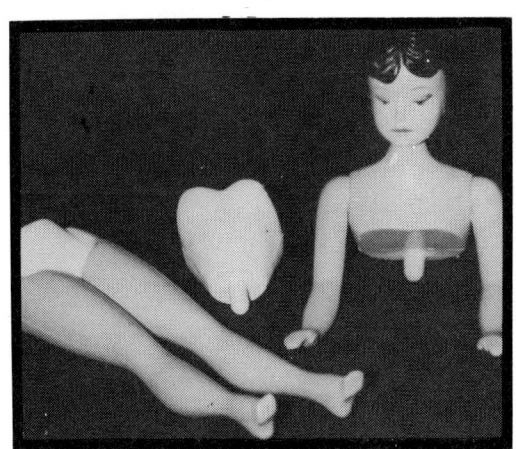

11" "PRINCESS PATTY". All rigid plastic. Blue lids/black molded lashes. Eyes painted white on black. Small lips. Red mohair. MARKS: none. Made in Canada. Courtesy Marie Ernst. $6.00

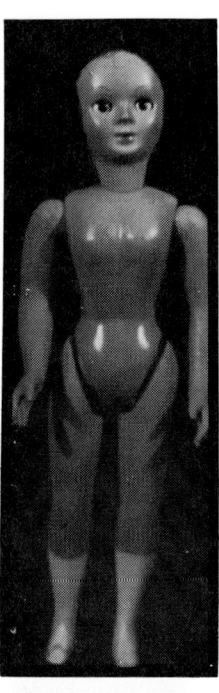

"RATTI" teenage doll. She is fully strung, of very early course plastic that is rough in texture except the body which is gray and smooth. Beautiful grey sleep eyes. Glued on wig with elaborate braids coiled around and glued over ears. Boots painted over toes that show. Courtesy Louise Ceglia. $6.00

12" "REAL MODEL". All hard plastic walker body. Jointed knees. Vinyl head. Sleep blue eyes. Replaced arms. MARKS: PMA, on head. PAT'S PEND, Lower back. 1956. $3.00

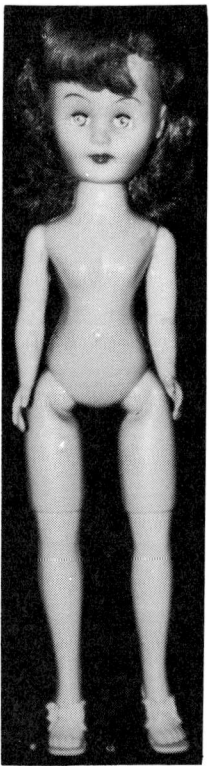

11½" "RENA". Plastic with vinyl head. Glued on yellow mohair wig. Painted eyes to side. Flat feet. 1965. by Grants Plastics. $4.00

11½" "SKYE", by Kenner. Jointed waist. Open/closed mouth with painted teeth. Very long neck. MARKS: 1975/.G.M.F.G.I., on head. 1974 GMFGI KENNER PROD./CINCINATTI, OHIO 45202/MADE IN HONG KONG, on lower back. Courtesy Phyllis Houston. Still Available

"SKYE", 1976 TRADE IN special by Kenner. Trade old doll and pay $1.99. The wrists are not jointed. Bathing suit is yellow with white/yellow flower. MARKS: 1975/G.M.F.G.L., on head. 1974. G.M. F.G.I. Kenner Prods./Cincinnati, Ohio 45202/Made in HONG KONG/G, on lower back. Gift from Joan Asherbraner. Still Available

12" "SUPERGIRL". All vinyl with wired legs and arms that are posable. Pale pink lips. Green eyes to the side. Green eyeliner. Black brows. MARKS: 1966/IDEAL TOY CORP/W-12-3, on head. 1965/IDEAL, in oval,/T-12 with a "1" lower on hip. TAG: 1967 IDEAL, in an oval, JAPAN. Courtesy Bev. Gardner. $22.00

12" "BLACK TAMMY". MARKS: 1965/2 IDEAL/T-12, on hip. 1964/IDEAL TOY CORP/T-12-E, on head. Original. $12.00

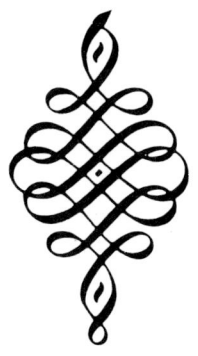

12" "TEENAGE DOLL", sold with trunk and wardrobe. 1963. Painted side glance eyes. Mary Poppins style body and limbs. Completely unmarked. Courtesy Phyllis Houston. $3.00

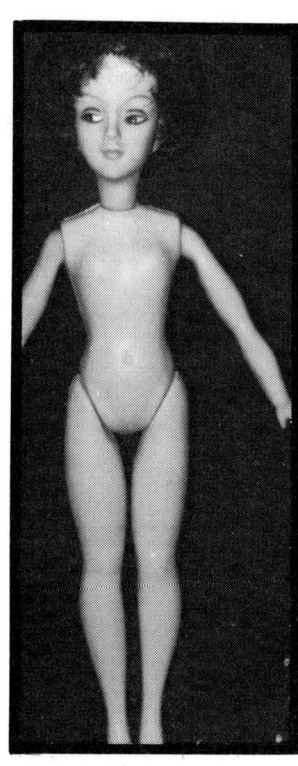

11¾" "BLACK TRESSY". Pale blue lined eyes & pale pink lips. Grow hair feature. Bendable knees. Shown with doll used "Mary Make Up". MARKS: AMER. DOLL & TOY CORP./1963 in circle, on head. Courtesy Marie Ernst. $12.00

11½" "TINA CASSINI". Rather yellow plastic boy & legs. Vinyl head and arms. Painted blue eyes to side. Black over & under liner. Medium high heels. MARKS: TINA CASSINI/MADE IN BRITISH/HONG KONG, on back. 1964. Came as blonde, white, black & brown hair. This outfit is called "EVENING STAR", gold threaded with white. TAG: MADE IN/BRITISH CROWN/COLONY OF/HONG KONG. Courtesy Joan Amundsen. $12.00

"TRESSY" Shown in outfit #25900 "Hootenanny". Light brown calf length pants. Black sweater. Brown shoes. Came with guitar, harmonica (marked "Tressy"), sheet music, book, vinyl bag and medallion. Courtesy Bessie Carson. $12.00

11¼" "TUESDAY TAYLOR". Rigid plastic body, rest vinyl. Bendable knees & arms. Jointed wrists. Inset lashes. Turn top of head to change color of hair. MARKS: 1975/Ideal, in oval, 4-248/Hong Kong, on head. Vertical on body: 1975 Ideal, in oval, U.S. Pat. No. 39003640/Hollis N.Y. 11423/Hong Kong P. Inset shows Black Tuesday Jones. Still Available.

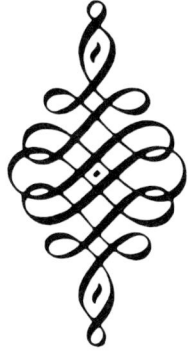

12½" "VIVIANA". Plastic and vinyl. Posable head. Sleep amber eyes/lashes. Open/closed mouth. Flat feet. Excellent hand detail. MARKS: ITALY/22, in square on torso. Tag: Zanini-Zambelli/Canneto Sull'oglio. Italy. Still Available

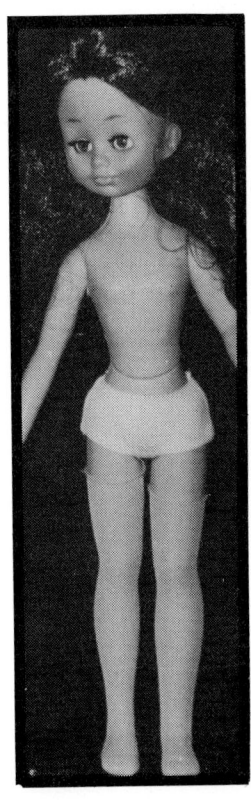

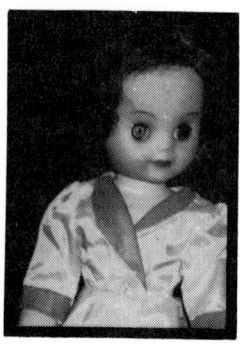

14" "TONI" by Ideal. Came in hard plastic and also all vinyl bodies. Glued on wig. Sleep eyes. MARKS: McCall Corp, on head. Hard plastic bodies marked: P-90. $20.00

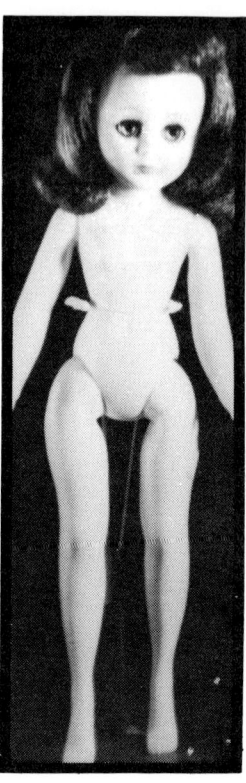

14" "TONI WALKER". To show body. Jointed waist. Pierced ears. Sleep blue eyes. High heels. Walker, head turns. MARKS: none. By American Character. $22.00

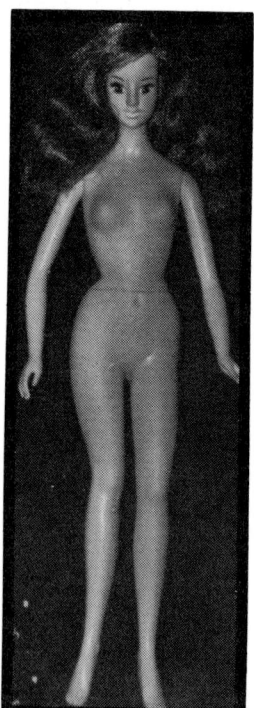

14" "BARBARA STREISAND". All excellent quality vinyl. Finger and toe detail is excellent also. Low jointed waist with 1 piece legs & torso. Large blue painted eyes. Large well molded nose. MARKS: none on doll. Dress tag MADE IN JAPAN. Courtesy Betty Tait. $35.00

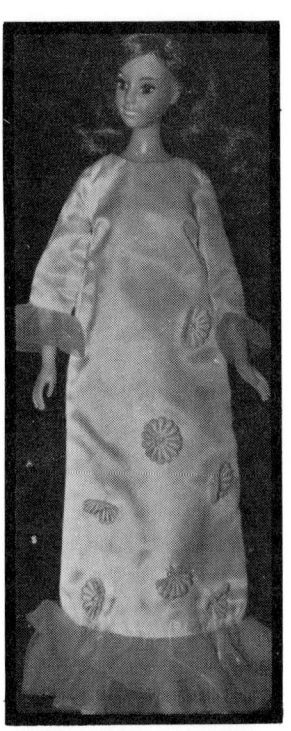

Shows the Original dress on the "BARBARA STREISAND" dolls. $35.00

Full face close up of 14" "BARBARA STREISAND".

Full profile of "BARBARA STREISAND DOLL". Excellent modeling, note the detail at base of neck.

12" "ACTION BUDDY". Hollow plastic body. Solid plastic legs. Solid vinyl arms. Only extra joints are knees. Molded dark brown hair & painted black eyes. MARKS: none. BOX: PENGO/INTERNATIONAL TOYS. Courtesy Marie Ernst.

11¼" "ADVENTURER" by Edico. 1974. Plastic with solid "wired" arms. Blue painted eyes, pink lips & molded brown hair. MARKS: MADE IN/HONG KONG, on back. Courtesy Bev. Gardner.

12" "ALL PRO-SPORTSMAN". Fully jointed including waist & ankles. MARKS: HONG KONG, on back. Made for Kresge.

9½" "ARCHIE & JUGHEAD". All vinyl. Bending knees. Jointed waist. MARKS: MADE IN HONG KONG/MARX INC., in circle/ARCHIE ENTERPRISES/INC. 1975.

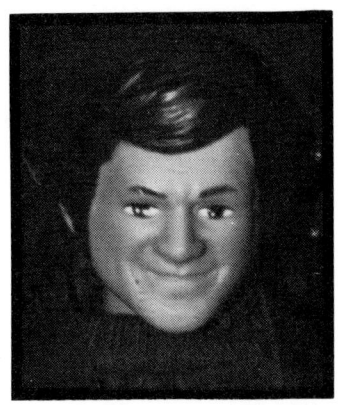

10" "J.J. ARMES". Full action figure with vinyl head. MARKS: Ideal, in oval, 1975/M-25, on head. B-59/Ideal, in oval, 1975/Made in Hong Kong P., on back.

12" "ATOMIC MAN-MIKE POWER". Propels self by rotating the hand held helicopter. Atomic flashing eye (one is inset & other painted). MARKS: G.I. JOE/COPYRIGHT 1964/ BY HASBRO/PAT. NO. 3277302/MADE IN USA, on back. HASBRO IND. INC. 1975/MADE IN HONG KONG, on head. Still available.

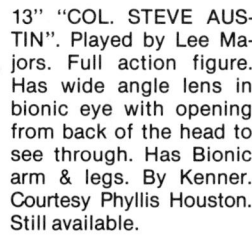

13" "COL. STEVE AUSTIN". Played by Lee Majors. Full action figure. Has wide angle lens in bionic eye with opening from back of the head to see through. Has Bionic arm & legs. By Kenner. Courtesy Phyllis Houston. Still available.

11½" "BIG RED". An exclusive with Wards. G.I. Joe type with painted on red beard. Hollow plastic upper arms. No extra joints. Suntan. MARKS: MADE IN/HONG KONG, on back. Courtesy Bev. Gardner.

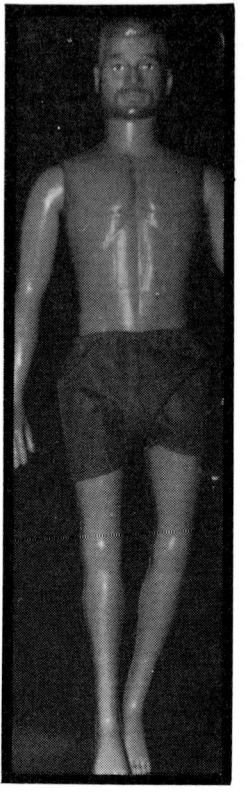

8" "BEN CARTRIGHT". All rigid vinyl. Extra joints at knees, elbows and wrists. MARKS: C/American Character, center of back. 1966.

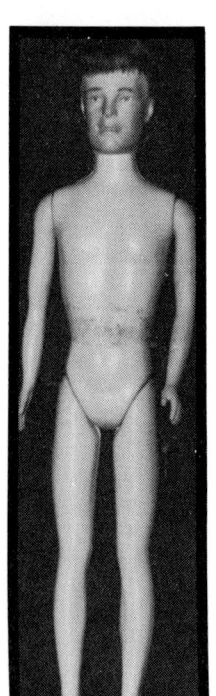

12" "BILL CHAMP". Cheap, lightweight plastic blonde version of "Chuck". Jointed waist, knees and ankles. MARKS: MADE IN HONG KONG, on back. By Totsy. Courtesy Joe Bourgious. $4.00

12½" "BILL". Plastic with solid vinyl arms. Vinyl head with painted brown eyes. Pink lips. Rooted over molded hair. MARKS: none. Made for Bella Hess Co. 1966. Courtesy Bev. Gardner. $4.00

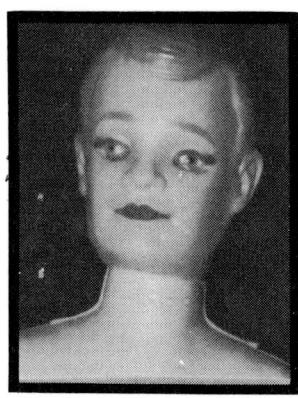

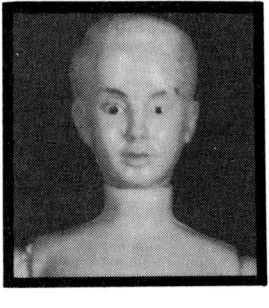

12" "BOB" and also "DON" (1964). Sold through Aldens. Boyfriend to Betty. Plastic & vinyl. Dark red lips. $2.00

11¾" "BOB". Very cheap plastic male doll. Arms are strung. Head and hips have the usual flange joints. Painted black eyes are almost crossed. Faint color in hair & lips. Prominent seams. Aldens 1964. Courtesy Phyllis Houston. $2.00

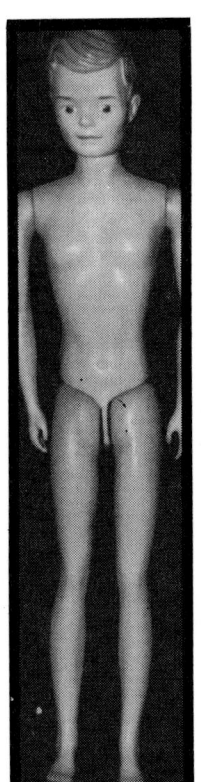

12" "BOB". Suzette's boyfriend. Light brown molded hair. Brown painted eyes. MARKS: UNEEDA DOLL CO. INC., in circle/1962, on back. $6.00

11¾" "BOBBY ORR". Thin arms and hands. No extra joints except waist. Soft plastic with vinyl head. Painted blue eyes. Open/closed mouth with painted teeth. MARKS: MADE IN/HONG KONG, on back. Made by Reliable of Canada. Courtesy Joe Bourgouis. Still Available

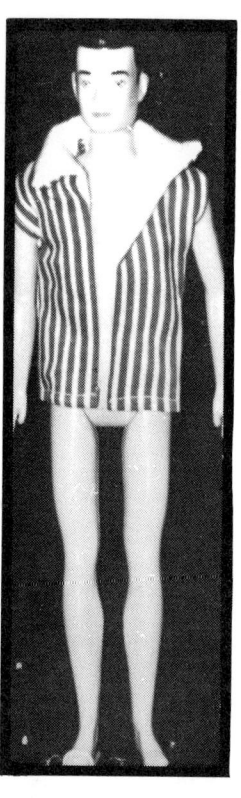

12" "BOY DOLL". Early Ken copy. Plastic with vinyl head. Black hair. Blue eyes with black dot in center and black iris. Courtesy Bev. Gardner.

10""BUTCH CAVANISH". Enemy to the Lone Ranger. Fully jointed. Excellent molding and quality of clothes. Boots missing. MARKS: 1973 LONE RANGER/TEL. INC/MADE IN HONG KONG/ FOR GABRIEL IND. INC.

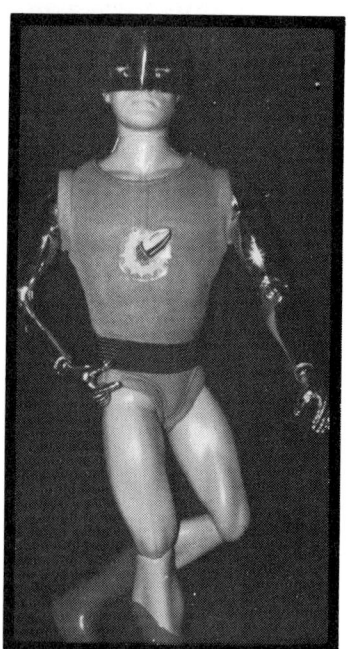

12" "BULLETMAN". The Human Bullet. A. G.I. Joe Adventure Team member. Full action figure. Molded on blue shorts that is lower torso. MARKS: 1975 / Hasbro / Pat. Pend. Pawt. R.I., on lower back. Removable "Bullet" cap. Courtesy Marie Ernst.

8" "CAPTAIN ACTION" and also boyfriend, "DON", for Dinah-mite. By Mego Corp.

8" "CAPT. HOOK". MARKS: LESNEY PRODUCTS/1973 Pat. Pend./ MADE IN HONG KONG/. $5.00

8" "CAPT. PEG-LEG" of the Fighting Furies. MARKS: LESNEY PRODUCTS/1973 Pat. Pend./ MADE IN HONG KONG.

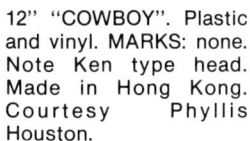

12" "COWBOY". Plastic and vinyl. MARKS: none. Note Ken type head. Made in Hong Kong. Courtesy Phyllis Houston.

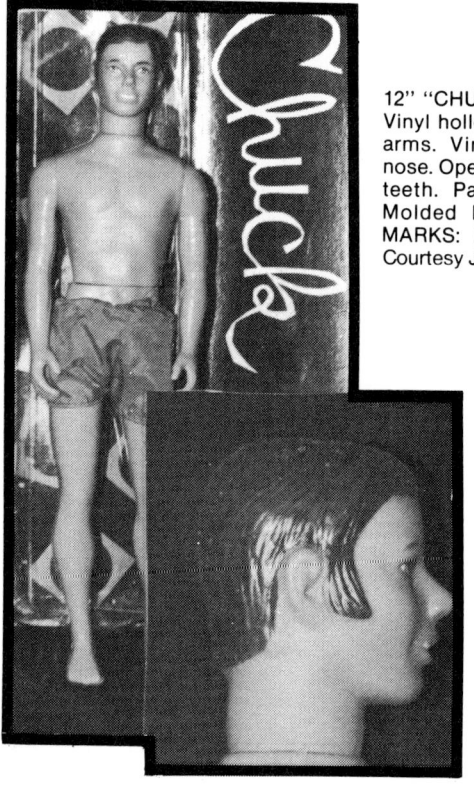

12" "CHUCK". Suntan. Jointed waist. Vinyl hollow legs with solid soft vinyl arms. Vinyl head with large sharp nose. Open/closed mouth with painted teeth. Painted blue eyes to front. Molded brow & long side burns. MARKS: HONG KONG, lower back. Courtesy Joe Bourgious.

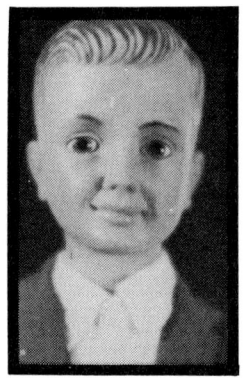

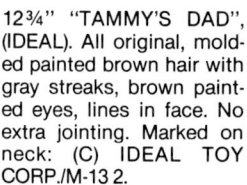

12¾" "TAMMY'S DAD", (IDEAL). All original, molded painted brown hair with gray streaks, brown painted eyes, lines in face. No extra jointing. Marked on neck: (C) IDEAL TOY CORP./M-13 2.

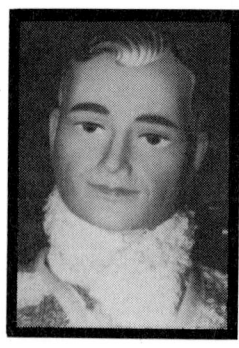

14½" Dad "DR. JOHN LITTLECHAP". Plastic & vinyl. MARKS: none. Remco. 1963.

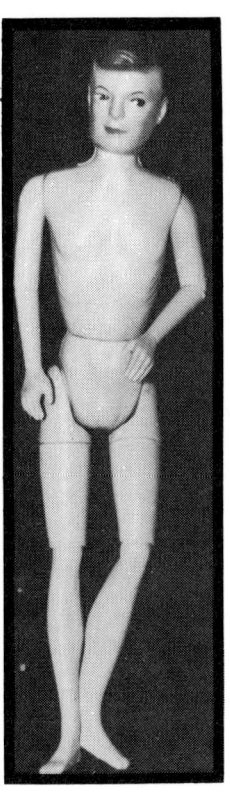

11¼" "DANNY POSE". Boyfriend to Debbie Pose. Plastic with vinyl head. Brown molded side part hair. Black painted eyes to side. Extra joints. MARKS: none. Courtesy Bev. Gardner.

8" "DAVID". All good quality vinyl. Flocked hair. Painted blue eyes. Original. MARKS: HONG KONG. Courtesy Marie Ernst.

11½" "THE DEFENDER". All rigid vinyl with vinyl head. Molded hair and painted eyes. No extra joints. MARKS: 1974/HASBRO IND. INC./PAWTUCKET R.I. 02861/MADE IN HONG KONG. Original. Extra outfits sold separately. Courtesy Phyllis Houston.

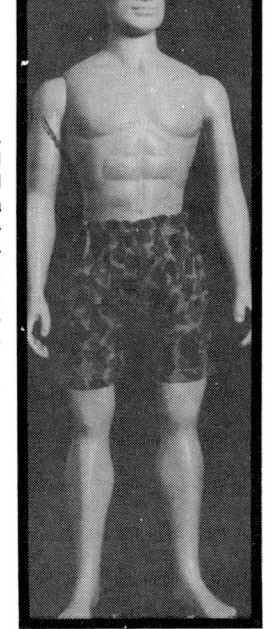

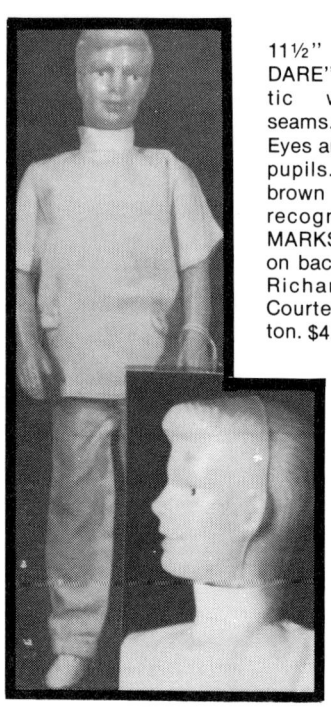

11½" "YOUNG DR. KILDARE". Very cheap plastic with prominent seams. Original clothes. Eyes are black with white pupils. Faint touch of brown on molded hair. A recognizable likeness. MARKS: HONG KONG, on back. Played by actor Richard Chamberlain. Courtesy Phyllis Houston. $4.00

9½" "DR. STEEL". Plastic and vinyl. Right "chopping" hand is silver. MARKS: MATTEL INC. 1974/HONG KONG, on head. 1971 MATTEL INC/U.S. & FOREIGN PATENTED/HONG KONG on back. Still available.

12" "FIGHTING ACE". Beige skin tones. Black hair. Painted eyes with blue rims. MARKS: MADE IN/HONG KONG/2012, on back. Made by Elite Creations.

12" "FIGHTING YANK". Jointed knees & ankles. One piece vinyl arms. Painted black hair & brown eyes. MARKS: MEGO CORP/MCMLXX & MINTEX, in diamond/TM/ MADE IN/HONG KONG. Courtesy Marie Ernst.

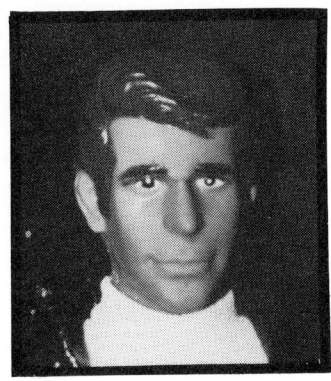

12" "GARY". Dark suntan. Hollow plastic legs, plastic arms & vinyl head. Jointed waist. Black eyes, open/closed mouth with painted teeth. MARKS: none. Maker unknown. Courtesy Joe Bourgious. $3.00

8" "FONZIE". Full action figure with vinyl head. Molded on blue shorts. MARKS: 1976 Paramount/Pictures Corp., on head. Mego Corp. 1976/Patents Pending/Made in Hong Kong, on back.

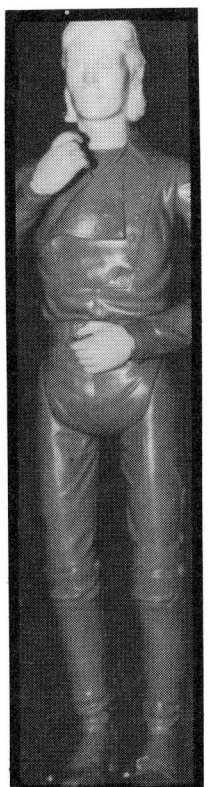

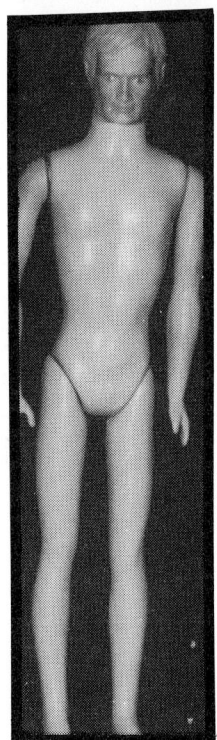

12" "ILLYA KURIYKIN". Plastic with vinyl arms & legs. Head made by Gilbert. MARKS: K71, on head. 2, on lower body. K-68 & K69 on arms. Courtesy Bev. Gardner.

12" "GENERAL CUSTER". All rigid vinyl. MARKS: Louis Marx & Co./MCMLXVIII/U.S.A.

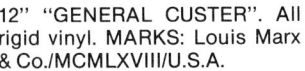

11½" "JED GIBSON". Molded on clothes & boots. Comes with 14 pieces of scout gear. MARKS: MARX TOY/M-CMLXXIII/MADE IN U.S.A., in circle at belt. Courtesy Phillis Houston.

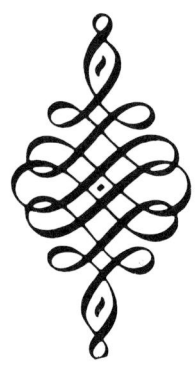

11½" "EAGLE EYE G.I. JOE". Full action figure with flocked beard. All fingers curled in "Kung Fu" grip. Molded on blue shorts (lower torso). Lever in back of head controls eyes. MARKS: HONG KONG, on head. 1975 Hasbro/Pat. Pend. Pawt. R. I., lower back. Courtesy Marie Ernst.

9½" "GOLD MEDAL BIG JIM". Comes with Gold Medal, Barbell Ball, Muscle band. Arm movement controlled by slot in back. Trunks are molded on. MARKS: MATTEL INC., on head. 1971 MATTEL INC./HONG KONG U.S.A./FOREIGN PATENTED, on hip. Still available.

12" "HAPPENING HANK". All vinyl. Molded red hair. Painted blue eyes. MARKS: HONG KONG, Head & back. Made by Peggy Ann Doll Clothes Inc. Courtesy Marie Ernst. $12.00

12" "JOHNNY HERO". Held football. By Rosko-Steele.

8" "KOJAK". Full action figure. MARKS: 1976 Universal/ City Studios Inc./1976 Excel Toy Corp/Made in Hong Kong.

10½" "MILITARY BOY". All hard plastic girls body with painted on black shoes. Man style hairdo painted on. Sleep blue/molded lashes. Wears part of original excellent quality uniform. MARKS: none.

12" "MOON McDARE". Plastic with solid vinyl arms. Vinyl head with "crew cut" molded hair. Painted brown eyes and wrinkled brow. Excellent ear detail. No extra joints. Made for Ideal by Gilbert. MARKS: G, on head. 2, on lower back. K-52 inside right arm, K86, left arm. Clothes tag: McDare/A.C. Gilbert Co./Japan. Courtesy Bev. Gardner.

6½" "MOUNTIE". Clothes are excellent quality. Comes with accessories which includes this Black/tan German Shepherd Dog. (Unmarked). $15.00.

6½" "MOUNTIE". Shows body construction. Feet are built into boots. Two screws in back hold top & bottom. Made of all rigid plastic. Has tiny inset blue eyes. Made by Madelman of Spain.

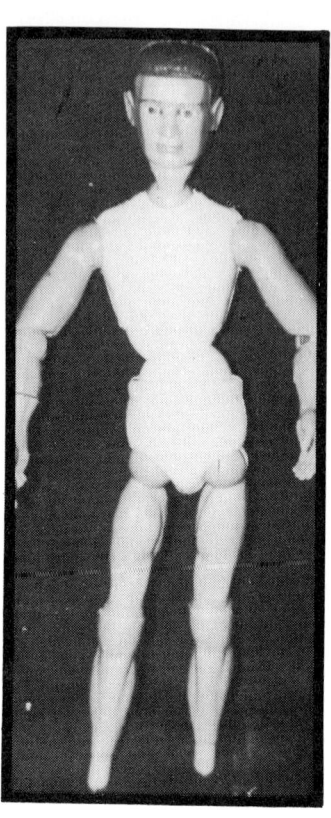

12" "MR. DOUBLE ACTION". Full jointed action figure. Plastic with vinyl head. Black painted eyes, beard. MARKS: none. By L.J.N.

8" "MR. MXYZPTKL". A Batman Arch-enemy. Mego.

12" "PAUL". Made by Fab-Lu-Ltd. Plastic with vinyl head. Light brown molded hair. Black painted eyes. MARKS: none. Made from the Dr. Ben Casey mold. Courtesy Marie Ernst. $3.00

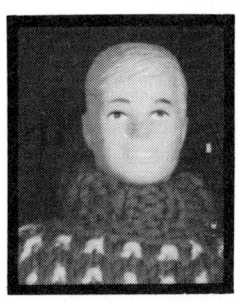

12" "POSIN' PAUL". Ken type with molded blonde hair. Eyes straight ahead. Action body and limbs are a pinkish shade, not suntan. Aldens. 1971. Courtesy Phyllis Houston. $3.00

12" "RANDY". Plastic & vinyl. Jointed waist. Molded brown hair. Painted blue eyes. Painted teeth. MARKS: MADE IN HONG KONG, center back. BOX: TOTSY/HOLYOKE, MASS. Courtesy Marie Ernst. $3.00

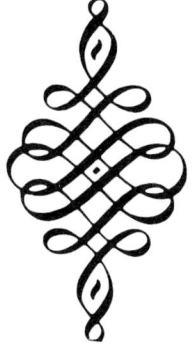

8" "THE RIDDLER". Batman Arch-enemy. Mego.

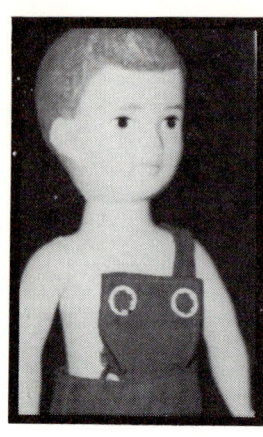

12" "ROGER". All better grade plastic. Flocked light brown hair. Painted blue eyes. MARKS: MADE IN JAPAN, on back.

9" O.J. SIMPSON". Full action figure with vinyl head. MARKS: Hong Kong, on torso, Shindana Toys/1975, on head.

9½" "SLADE". Super Agent. Plastic with vinyl head. Full action figure. Excellent head detail. MARKS: SHINDANA TOYS/1976, on head. Hong Kong, on body. Courtesy Phyllis Houston.

12½" "SONNY". Excellent quality plastic & vinyl. Bending knees. Action figure except not jointed ankles. MARKS: Mego Corp. 1976, on head. Mego Corp. 1976/Made in Hong Kong, on back.

12" "JOHNNY STRONG" by Mor-Toys, made in Hong-Kong. No date given. Inexpensive plastic with vinyl flexible arms, jointed knee, hip, shoulder; swivel waist and head. This is No. 8005. Doll came in three other sets. Marked on back: Made in Hong Kong.

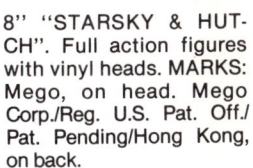

8" "STARSKY & HUTCH". Full action figures with vinyl heads. MARKS: Mego, on head. Mego Corp./Reg. U.S. Pat. Off./Pat. Pending/Hong Kong, on back.

8" "MIGHTY THOR". A Super Hero. Full action figure with rooted hair. Hole in top of head to fit silver helmet. MARKS: 1975 Marvel/C.G., on head. Mego Corp. 1974/Reg. U.S. Pat. Off./Pat. Pending/Hong Kong. Courtesy Marie Ernst.

11½" "TONI". Hollow plastic legs and arms. Vinyl head with molded dark hair. Painted blue eyes to front. Original red/white leisure suit. MARKS: MADE IN/HONG KONG, upper back. No information on pack. Courtesy Marie Ernst. $2.00

12" "VILLAIN". All rigid vinyl. MARKS: MARX TOYS, in a circle.

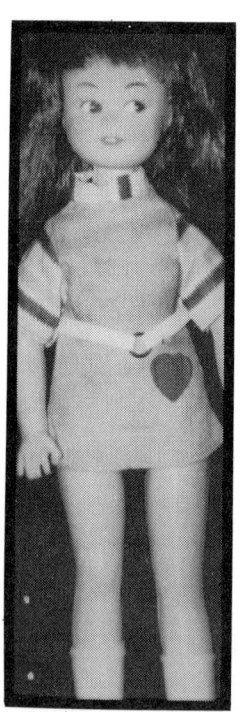

9" "CANDI". Plastic with vinyl head. Eyes painted to left. Dimples. Original. MARKS: None. $6.00

6¼" "CARLA". All vinyl, bendable and posable. Tutti's friend #7377. Box: 1973. MARKS: 1965/Mattel Inc./ Hong Kong, on lower back. Courtesy Marie Ernst. Sold in Europe.

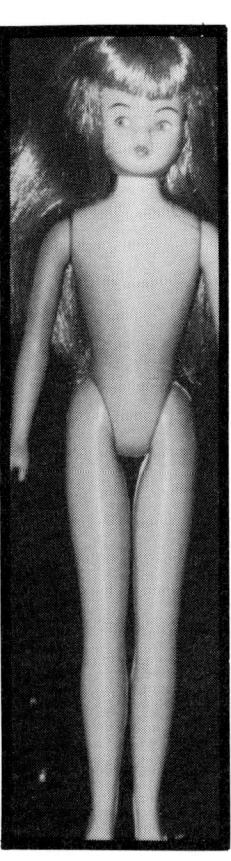

8½" "DOTTIE". Imitation Penny Brite, has orange rooted hair, black side glancing eyes white highlight, dimples, and clothes are original. Very cheap plastic, marked on shoulders made in/Hong Kong.

9" "DORIS" by Prima. Plastic with solid thin vinyl arms. Vinyl head with long rooted hair. Small painted blue eyes to the side. Flat feet. MARKS: PRIMA, on head. Courtesy Bev. Gardner.

9" "KID SISTER". Plastic & vinyl. Freckles. MARKS: EEGEE CO./32.

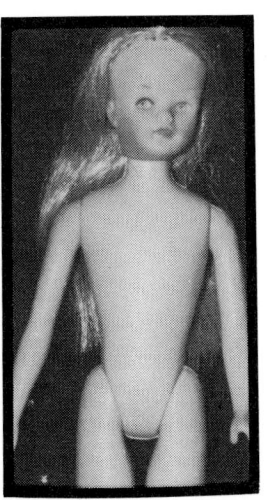

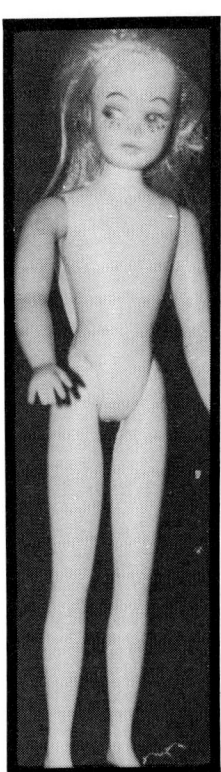

9½" "JUNIOR MISS". Also sold as "MARTY". Good quality plastic & vinyl. Small painted blue eyes. Small hole in crown. MARKS: AE/1964, on head.

8" "LITTLE LAURIE". Brown painted eyes to side. Painted teeth. Plastic & vinyl. MARKS: MADE IN HONG KONG. BOX: AMSCO TOYS/NEW YORK N.Y. Courtesy Marie Ernst. This same furniture was sold as DAWN'S (DELUXE) also.

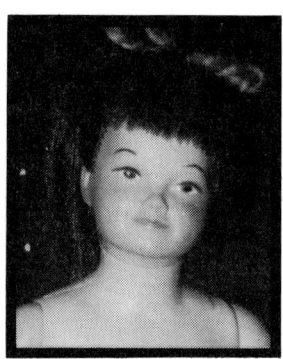

10½" "LIBBIE LITTLECHAP". Plastic and vinyl. MARKS: Libby Littlechap/Remco Ind. 1963.

9½" "LOLA BALLERINA". Plastic body with rigid plastic legs, right leg slightly bent. Solid vinyl arms, left slightly bent with cupped hand. Vinyl head fits into body. Large green painted eyes, painted lashes around eyes. Brown eyeshadow with purple wash over eyes. Thick rooted hair. Excellent molded protruding ears. MARKS: MADE IN HONG KONG. By Deluxe, Germany. Courtesy Bev. Gardner.

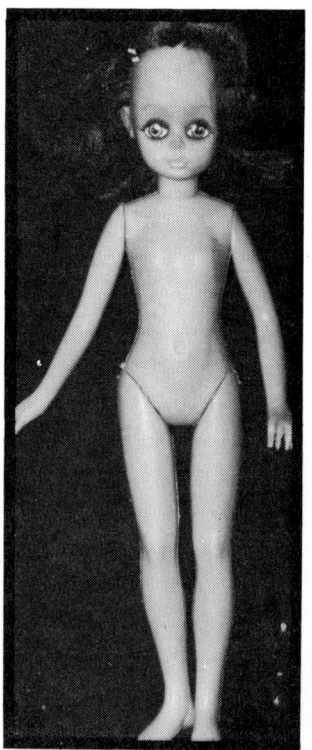

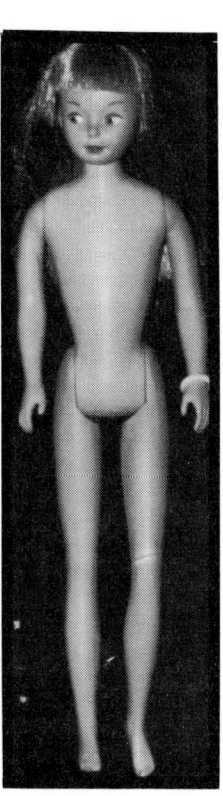

9" "MARY LOU". Plastic with vinyl head and limbs. Wired and posable legs. Green painted eyes to side. MARKS: AMER. CHAR./1964, on head. Courtesy Joe Bougious.

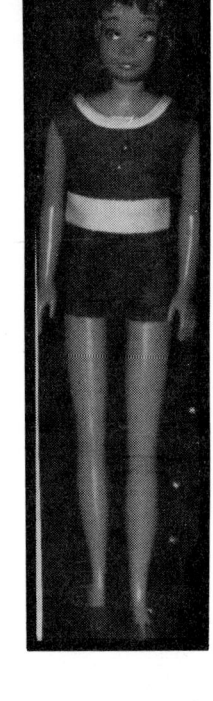

9" "MISS PRE-TEEN" U.S.A. Plastic with vinyl head. Painted blue eyes. Original. MARKS: MADE IN/HONG KONG, on back. Has odd, rather beige colored plastic. Made by Princess Grace Doll Co. a part of Mego Corp.

8½" "PENNY SWEET". Plastic with solid vinyl arms. Vinyl head with painted solid black eyes & lashes. "ooh" type closed mouth. Rooted hair. MARKS: PENNY SWEET/PERFECTA/HONG KONG, on head. MADE IN/HONG KONG, on back. Courtesy Bev. Gardner.

Our Gang members. Darla & Alfalfa. He is full action figure and she is all vinyl with bending knees. MARKS: 1975/M.G.M. Inc., on head. Mego Corp 1975/Reg. U. S. Pat. Off/Pat. Pending/Hong Kong, on back. Courtesy Marie Ernst.

Our Gang members, Spanky, Buckwheat & Micky. Full action figures. MARKS: 1975/M.G.M. Inc., on head. Mego corp. 1975/Reg. U.S. Pat. Off/Pat. Pending/Hong Kong, on back. Courtesy Marie Ernst.

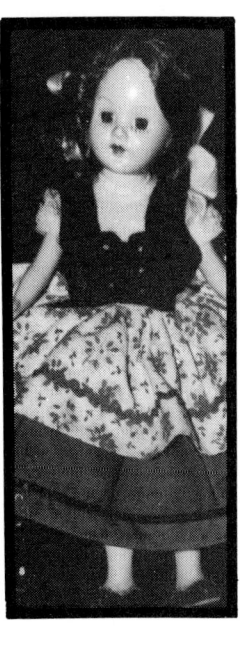

8" "SANDRA SUE". All excellent quality hard plastic. Walker. Sleep eyes/molded lashes. Flat feet. Original outfit. MARKS: none. Made by Richwood. $12.00

9" "SANDY". Plastic with vinyl head. Jointed neck, shoulders & hips. Painted eyes. MARKS: UNIQUE/1965. Made for Elite. Courtesy Phillis Houston.

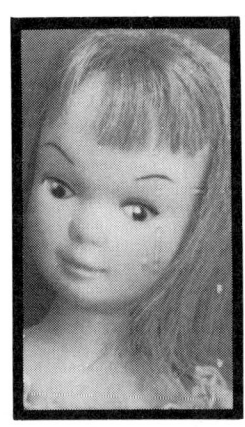

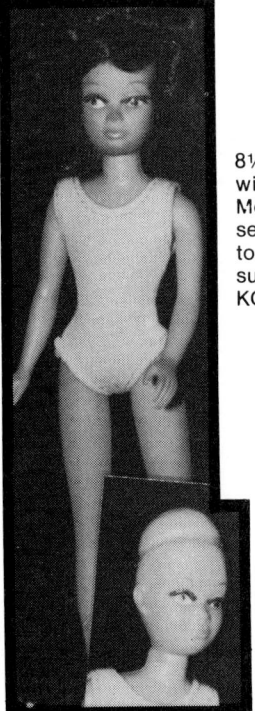

8½" "POSIN' SANDY". All vinyl with wired legs for posing. Molded hair to take wigs. Long set in lashes. Painted blue eyes to side. Flat feet. Original pink suit. MARKS: MADE IN/HONG KONG. Courtesy Bev Gardner.

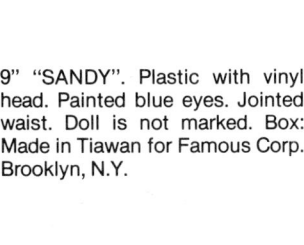

9" "SANDY". Plastic with vinyl head. Painted blue eyes. Jointed waist. Doll is not marked. Box: Made in Tiawan for Famous Corp. Brooklyn, N.Y.

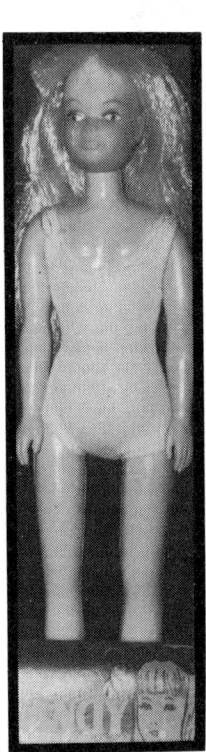

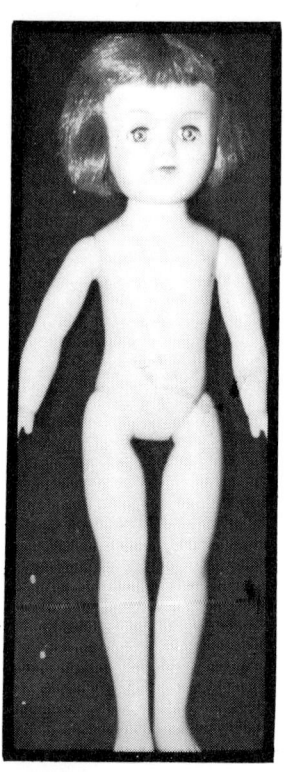

10" "SHIRLEY ANN". All excellent quality vinyl. Dimples. Flat feet. Made by Ideal on very limited basis. MARKS: 10, on back. $15.00

10" "SHIRLEY TEMPLE". (Also 12"). All good quality vinyl with rooted hair, sleep eyes with molded lashes. Flat feet. Pre-teen figure. $25.00

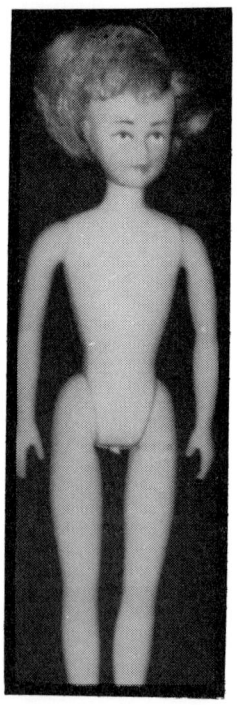

9" "VANITY". Plastic body with vinyl head & limbs. Painted blue eyes, brown pupils. MARKS: MADE IN HONG KONG/MARX/TOYS, in circle. $2.00

8½" "WONDER DOLL". Thin plastic with solid vinyl arms. Vinyl head with painted blue eyes to side/inset long lashes & green eyeshadow. Rooted yellow hair. Jointed waist and flat feet. Original. MARKS: HONG KONG, on back. Package: JAK PAK/Milwaukee U.S.A. Courtesy Bev. Gardner. $2.00

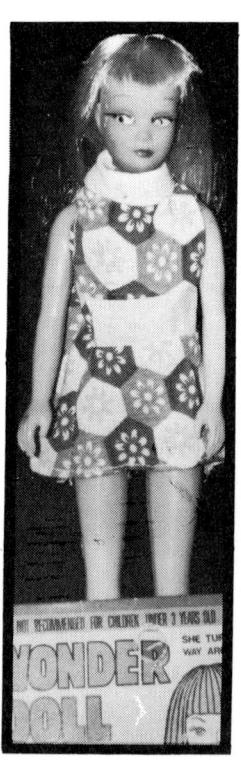

"HAPPY FAMILY" Same as Vol. III but has different clothes. Box: Made for Woolworth. Courtesy Phyllis Houston.

10", 9¾" & 3½" Fashion Doll Family. "THE HAPPY FAMILY". Ward's exclusive 1976. Marks: Made in Hong Kong, on backs. All are plastic with vinyl head and have no extra joints. Baby has jointed neck only.

"MICHAEL & MELINDA". Young Sweethearts by Mattel. Full action figures. Excellent quality dolls & clothes.

Alexander's all composition "Dr. Devoe" checks out Barbie and says, "They didn't look like that when I was going to school!" Courtesy Ruby K. Arnold.

Serious Barbie and family collectors should refer to the book, "BARBIE DOLLS" by Sibyl DeWein and Joan Ashabraner. This section on Mattel teens is included only because Barbie is part of the entire teen "scene". Collector's are also referred to Vol. II and Vol. III of "Modern Collector's Dolls". Current prices of "The Barbie Family" will be found in the above books.

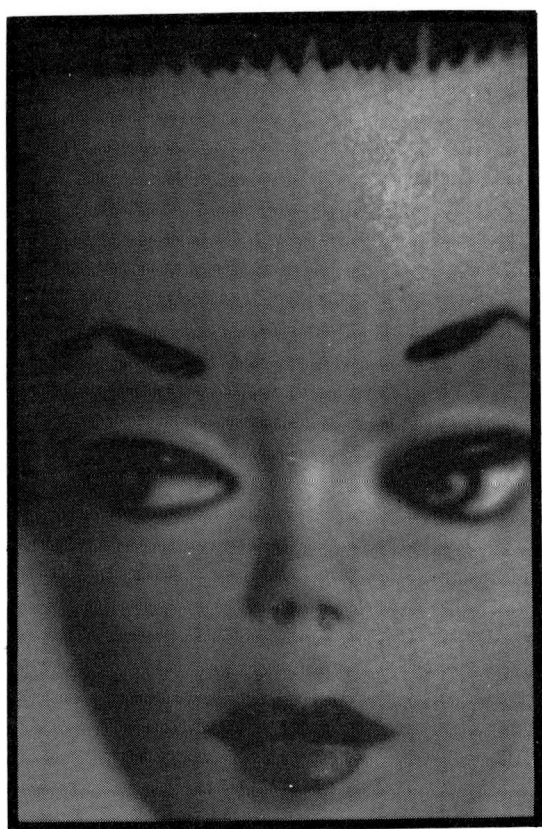

"#1 Barbie" (#850). Iris of eyes are white and eyebrows are peaked. Lipstick & nails are very dark red. Has holes in feet for stand. MARKS: Barbie/Pat's. Pend. MCM-LVIII/by/Mattel/Inc. 1959. Courtesy Sarah Sink.

#2 "BARBIE" (#850). Basically the same doll as the #1 Barbie but has no holes in feet for stand. Ponytail with curly bangs. Heavy, solid torso. Marked same as #1. Dark red lips and nails.

**ILLUSTRATIONS NOT AVAILABLE**

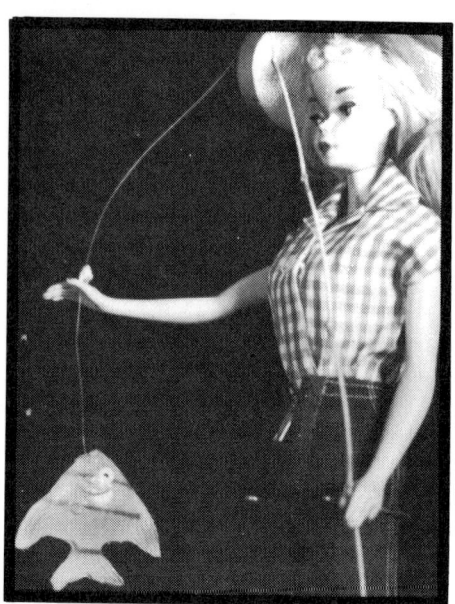

#3, #850, "BARBIE". Brown eyeshadow. In #0967 picnic set. This set is the second set which has a different hat, bag and color of fish. The first fish was yellow & orange and this second issue one is blue & green. 1960. Courtesy Phyllis Houston.

#4 "BARBIE". Soft, heavy body of new material that didn't turn light colored. Ponytail, with tight bangs. Dark red lips & nails. Blue iris. Still model number 850. 1961. Marked with the "Pat's Pend" mark. Courtesy Phyllis Houston.

11½" #5 "PONYTAIL BARBIE". Red hair with one row rooted pulled through bangs. MARKS: Barbie/Pat. Pend/MC-MLVIII/Mattel/Inc. Japan, on right foot. 2, on left hip. (#850) 1961. The firm texture of the bangs indicates a #5 doll. Courtesy of Mary Partridge.

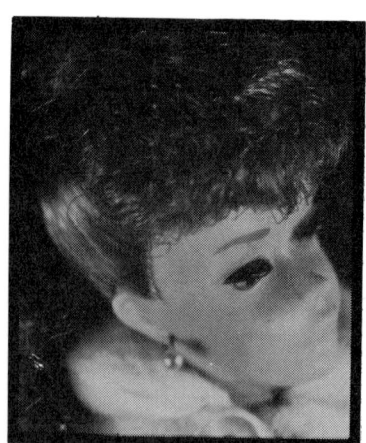

#7 "BARBIE". Ponytail. Hard, hollow "Pat. Pend." body. 1962. (#850).

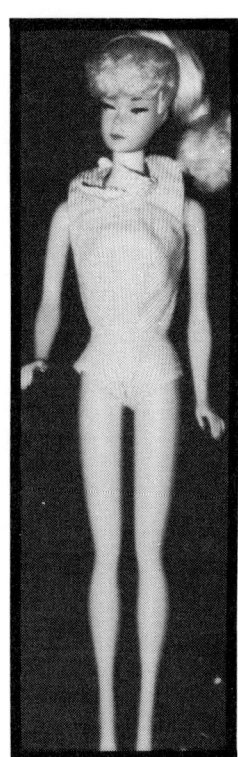

#6 (#850) "BARBIE" by Mattel. First bubblecut Barbie with black hair is almost an afro. Green eyeshadow, dark red lips and nails. She wears #0961, Evening Splendor. On hip: Barbie R/Pat. Pend./MCMLVIII/by/Mattel/Inc. On right foot: Japan. Ca. 1961.

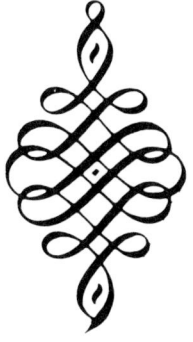

11½" #8 "BUBBLECUT BARBIE". Looser red hairdo. Brown eyeshadow. Dark red lips & nails. Original earrings. MARKS: Barbie/Pat. Pend./MCMLVIII/by Mattel/Inc. Japan, on right foot. (#850). 1962. Courtesy Mary Partridge.

#9 "BARBIE". Model #0850. Ponytail.

**ILLUSTRATIONS NOT AVAILABLE**

11½" "BUBBLECUT BARBIE". Paler lips and nails. #0850. Very light eyeshadow. "Pierced ears". MARKS: MIDGE TM/1962/BARBIE/1958/by/Mattel Inc. Japan, on bottom of right foot. (#0850). Courtesy Mary Partridge. 1963.

11" "BARBIE". Fashion Queen with molded hair and band plus wigs. Came in gold/white striped suit and head scarf. On "MIDGE" marked body. (#0870). MARKS: Midge/1962/Barbie (R)/1958/by/ Mattel Inc. Courtesy Phyllis Houston.

# 12 "BARBIE". (#850). Swirl bangs that are rooted deep into the forehead. Original set is across the forehead to the side and into the ponytail. Came in one piece red suit. Few on "Pat. Pend." bodies but most on Midge marked ones.

#13 "MISS BARBIE". Sleep eyes. Molded hair with wigs. On "MIDGE" marked body. (#1060). Courtesy Phyllis Houston.

#14 "BARBIE". Side part, hairband and bending knees. Model #1070. 1966. (#1070) 3 hair styles. Courtesy Sarah Sink.

#15. 11½" "BARBIE". Color magic #1150. Light blue lined eyes and blue eyeshadow. Red lips and nails. Bendable knees. Bright yellow straw like hair. MARKS: 1958/Mattel Inc./U.S. Patented/U.S. Pat. Pend./Made in Japan. 5, on left hip. Courtesy Mary Partridge.

#16 "BARBIE". (#1160). Twist 'n Turn. Long hair. Set in eyelashes. Bendable legs. Jointed waist.

#17 "BARBIE". (#1190). Straight legs and painted eyelashes. In 2 piece pink suit. Courtesy Sarah Sink.

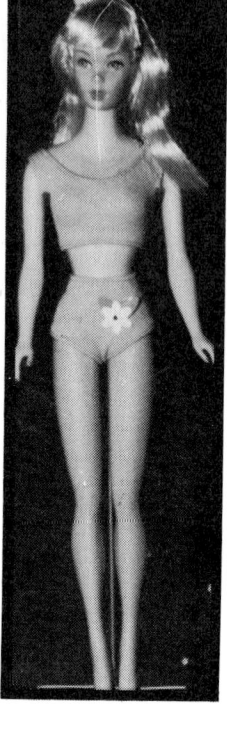

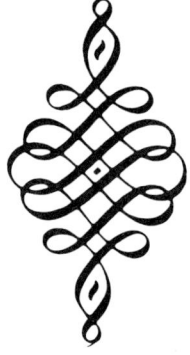

#18 "Barbie". (#4042). Hair fair. Blue eyes to side with inset lashes. Open/closed mouth. Jointed waist & bend knees. MARKS: 1966/Mattel Inc./U.S. Patented/U.S. Pat. Pend./Made in Japan. 10, on left hip. Courtesy Mary Partridge.

#19 "TALKING BARBIE." Model #1115. Curls at nape of neck. Also Spanish speaking Barbie (#8348 with Stacey head mold).

**ILLUSTRATIONS NOT AVAILABLE**

#22 "BARBIE". (#1155 & 1152). Live action. Blue eyes ahead with inset lashes. Open/closed mouth. Full posable body. Courtesy Mary Partridge.

#20. 11½" "DRAMATIC NEW LIVING BARBIE" #1116. Blue eyes to side with inset lashes. Open/closed mouth. Jointed waist and wrists. Bendable elbows and knees. MARKS: 1968 Mattel Inc./ U.S. & For. Pat'd/Other Pats. Pend./Taiwan. Issued 1970. Courtesy Mary Partridge.

#24 "BARBIE". Hair Happenin's. Jointed waist, bend legs, blue eyes, inset lashes. Short red hair and 3 hair pieces. Model #1174. Courtesy Sarah Sink.

#23 "MALIBU BARBIE". Model #1067.

#25 "BARBIE". Growin' Pretty hair. Blue eyes ahead. Jointed waist, bend knees. Hole in head for hair pieces. MARKS: 1967 Mattel Inc./U.S. Patented/ Other Patents Pend./Patented in Canada 1967/Taiwan. Model number 1144. Courtesy Mary Partridge.

#26 is the "WALK LIVELY BARBIE". Model #1182.

#27 "BARBIE". Busy model #3311.

**ILLUSTRATIONS NOT AVAILABLE**

#28 "TALKING BUSY BARBIE". Model #1195.

**ILLUSTRATIONS NOT AVAILABLE**

#29 is the Ward's Anniversary doll. A re-issue of the original "BARBIE". Model #3210.

#30 is model #4220, the original "QUICK CURL BARBIE".

#31 "SWEET 16 BARBIE". Blue eyes ahead with three heavy painted lashes. Open/closed mouth. Jointed waist and bendable knees. Model #7796. Courtesy Phyllis Houston.

#32 is the "SUN VALLEY BARBIE" model #7806. It is the same face as the Newport Barbie.

11½" "BALLERINA BARBIE", by Mattel. Ca. 1976, all original. Doll has posing stand. Painted eyes, rooted fine blonde hair, snapping knee. Marked just above swivel waist: (C) MATTEL, Inc. 1966/ U.S. Patent Pending/TAIWAN. #30.

11½" "GOLD MEDAL BARBIE". Regular suntan Barbie. Jointed waist. Suit is untagged. MARKS: 1966/ MATTEL INC/US & FOREIGN/PATENTED/OTHER PATS. / PENDING / MADE IN/TAIWAN.

11½" #36 "HAWAIIAN BARBIE". #7470. Suntan with rigid plastic body, solid feeling vinyl legs and arms. Bending knees. Black rooted hair and brown painted eyes. Deep almost purple lips. MARKS: 1966/Mattel Inc./ U.S. Patented/U.S. Pat. Pend./Made in Korea, lower hip. 9, on other hip. Accessories marked 1973/ Mattel. Courtesy Bev. Gardner.

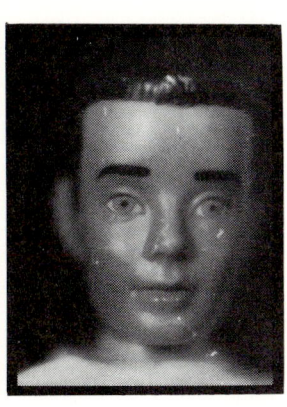
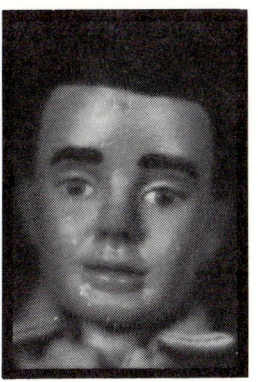

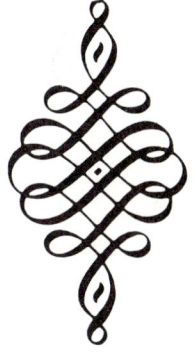

This page shows the changes in the face of "KEN". First had "crew cut" painted, second had flocked hair.

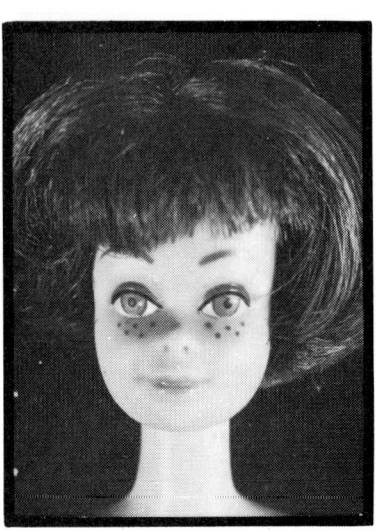

9¼" "SKIPPER". All rigid plastic and vinyl. Brown eyes to side. Freckles. Smile mouth. MARKS: 1963/Mattel Inc. on hip vertically. 5, on left hip. Japan on sole of foot. Courtesy Mary Partridge.

11½" "MIDGE". Blue eyes ahead. Brown eyeliner. Freckles. Bendable knees. Small waist and very "hippy". Large busts. MARKS: 1958/Mattel Inc./U.S. Patented/ U.S. Pat. Pending/Made in Japan. 2, on left hip. Courtesy Mary Partridge.

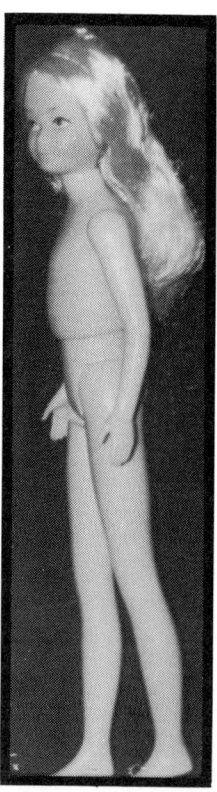

9" MATTEL'S "POSE'N' PLAY SKIPPER". Jointed waist. Bending knees. Came in clear plastic bag. Blue and white checked playsuit. No shoes. Stock No. 1117. Ca. 1974. Courtesy Phyllis Houston.

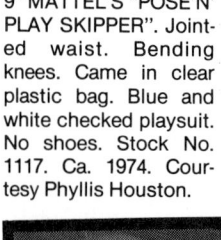

Shows side view of "Growing Up Skipper" as a little girl.

"FRANCIE". First is #1100 Black Francie, followed by first face, Hair Happenings, with painted lashes and inset lashes. Black Francie courtesy of Sarah Sink. Remainder courtesy of Phyllis Houston.

"TUTTI". Me & My Dog set #3554. Brunette "TUTTI" Red coat with fur trim, fur cap, leotards & big dog on red leash. Courtesy Sarah Sink.

"TUTTI". Night night Sleep Tight Set #3553. Ash blonde "TUTTI" in floral robe that matches bedspread. White bed. Courtesy Sarah Sink.

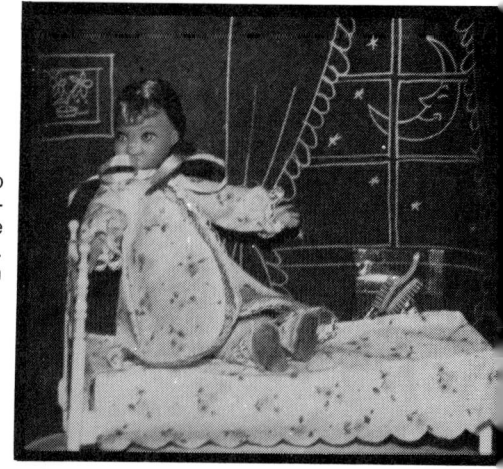

"TUTTI". Walking My Dolly Set #3552. Red & white dress, straw hat. Ash blonde hair. Courtesy Sarah Sink.

"TUTTI & TODD". Sundae Treat Set #3556. Both have red hair. Outfits match and are red/white & blue. Chairs and table are pink and in one unit. Courtesy Sarah Sink.

"TUTTI". Melody in Pink Set #3555. Pink frilly dress, orange piano & stool. Pale blonde. Courtesy Sarah Sink.

"TUTTI". Cookin' Goodies Set #3559. Brunette updo. Stove is white trimed in pink with "TUTTI" on front of stove. Courtesy Sarah Sink.

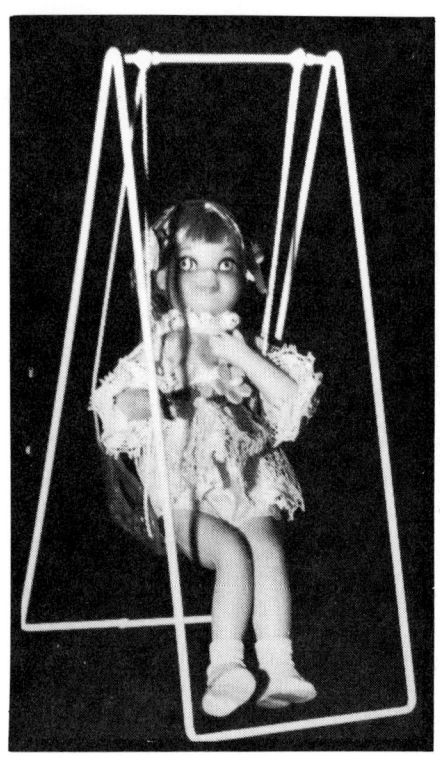

"TUTTI". Swing A Ling Set #3560. Ash blonde. Courtesy Sarah Sink. Under $1.00

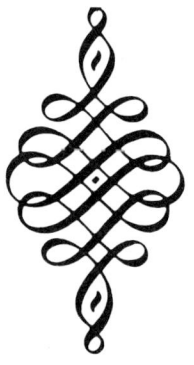

6¼" "CARLA", Tutti's friend. #7377. 1973. All vinyl that is bendable & posable. Courtesy Marie Ernst. Under $1.00

11" "CASEY". Francie's friend. 1967 model #1180. Short hair and bendable legs. Courtesy Phyllis Houston.

"TWIGGY". #1185. Very short hair & much eye makeup. Courtesy Phyllis Houston.

"TWIGGY & CASEY". Same doll except for hair & eye treatment. Courtesy Phyllis Houston.

11¼" "CASEY" by MATTEL. Straight legs of shiny plastic. Blonde hair & brown eyes. Hot pink bathing suit. Came in plastic clear bag. Stock No. 9000*. Ca. 1974. (Note Francie face). Courtesy Phyllis Houston.

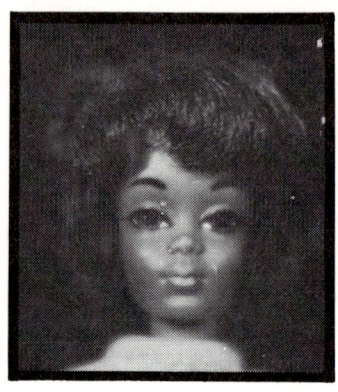

"CHRISTIE". #1125 Talking and #1165 Twist N Turn. Courtesy Phyllis Houston.

11½" "STACEY". Blue eyes ahead with inset lashes. Open/closed mouth with painted teeth. Jointed waist. Red hair. Bendable knees. MARKS: 1966/Mattel Inc./U.S. Patented/U.S. Pat. Pend./Made in/Japan. 4, on left hip. Courtesy Mary Partridge.

11½" "TRULY SCRUMPTIOUS". #1107, 1969. Talking. #1108 had straight legs. Courtesy Phyllis Houston.

"JULIA". First issue doll #1127. Nurse. Courtesy Phyllis Houston.

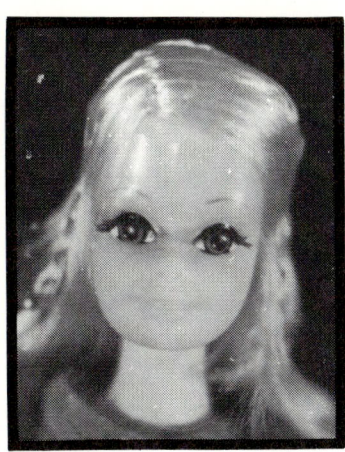

"LIVE ACTION P. J." Inset lashes. Tiny braids in hair. 1971

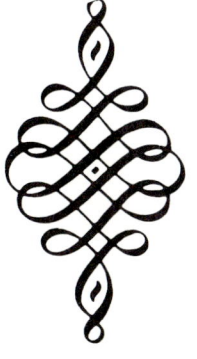

1976 "OLYMPIC BARBIE." Red/white/blue suit with Gold Medal.

12" "TALKING BRAD." MARK: 1968 Mattel, on hip. 1969, on head.

"BAGGIE BARBIE." Sold during 1975 in plastic bag. Also packaged this way were Casey and Francie.

9¼" "FLUFF". #1143 made in 1971. Courtesy Phyllis Houston.

9" "TIFF". All vinyl with dark red rooted hair. Brown painted eyes. Closed smile mouth. All original. Made by Mattel in 1972. Courtesy Phyllis Houston.

11½" "STEFFIE". #1183 Walk Lively, #3312 Busy. 1972-73. Courtesy Phyllis Houston.

"KELLEY QUICK CURL". #4221, 1973 and Yellowstone #7808, 1974. Courtesy Phyllis Houston.

"GROWING UP GINGER". Turn her left arm counter clockwise and she grows from 9" to 9¾" tall and bosom grows. Long brown hair is parted on side and tied up in back. Brown painted eyes. Serious face. Marked on hip: (C) 1967/ Mattel, Inc/Hong Kong/ US & FOR PAT/Patented Canada/1974.

11½" "CARA BALLERINA". Knob crown built into head. 1976. Courtesy Phyllis Houston.

"DELUXE QUICK CURL CARA", 11½". All original Medium brown hair, light brown eyes, yellow dress, has extra lock of hair and grooming pieces in box. Stock No. 9219. (Unbelievably this doll has no pants.) On hip: (C) 1965/Mattel Inc/ U.S. & Foreign/Patented/ Other Pts. /Pending/Made in/Taiwan - Knees snap. ($4.96)

11½" "FREE MOVING CARA" and 12" "FREE MOVING CURTIS". Made by Mattel. All original, dressed in orange and white. Both have painted brown eyes. His hair is molded and painted; hers is dark brown, rooted. Vinyl and plastic. Stock Nos. 7283 and 7282. Ca. 1975. MARKED on Hip: (C) 1967 Mattel Inc/Taiwan/U.S. Pat. Pend. (Cara): (C) 1968 MATTEL, INC./ Taiwan/U.S. Patent/ Pending (Curtis). Both are fully jointed with snapping knees and swivel waists.

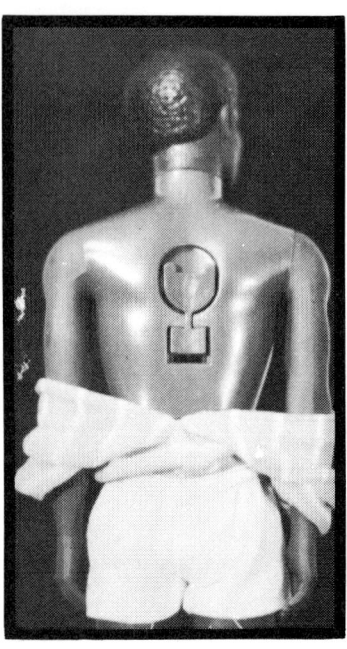

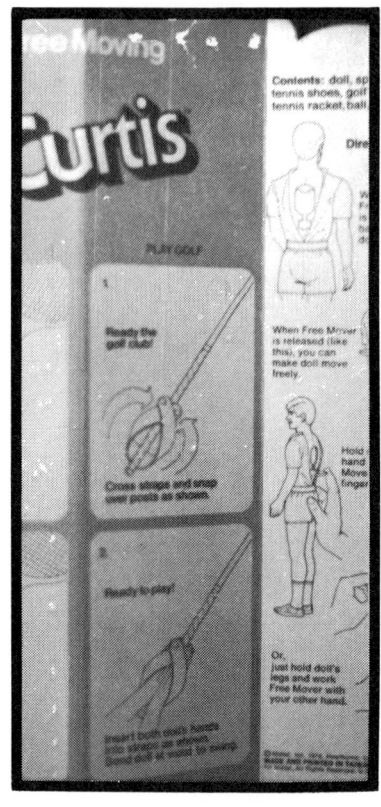

"FREE MOVING CURTIS". Shows mechanism in back. Courtesy Phyllis Houston.

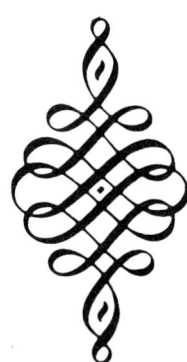

"DRESSED DOLL". Mattel box has a blue end and a blue band across it. This means the doll that came in the box was dressed in an outfit other than a bathing suit. Courtesy Marie Ernst.

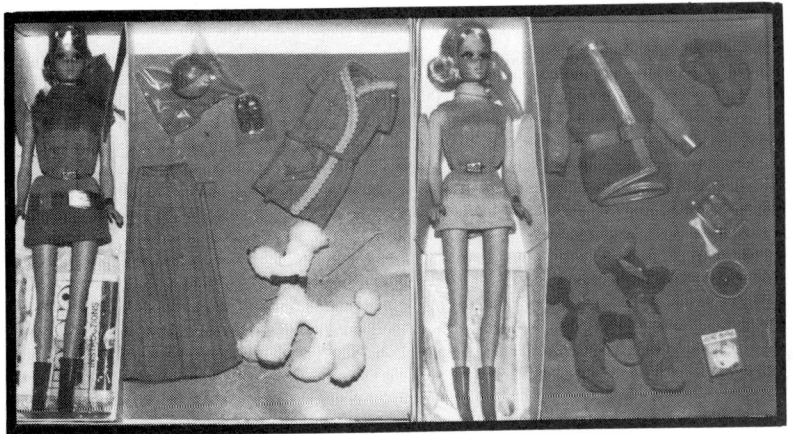

Sear's two versions of "WALKING JAMIE" and white & grey dogs.
Courtesy of Sarah Sink.

"BARBIE"' Sparkling Pink gift set #1011 - 1963. Courtesy Sarah Sink.

Dramatic New Living "BARBIE" Action Accents gift set. Courtesy Sarah Sink.

Talking "BARBIE" Pink Premiere gift set. Courtesy Sarah Sink.

1961

1962
Blue
&
Yellow
Covers

4 Booklets
for
1963

 1964

 1966

 1967

1968

1969

1971

1970